Lismore
The Great Garden

Lismore
The Great Garden

ROBERT HAY

BIRLINN

First published in 2009 by
Birlinn Limited
West Newington House
10 Newington Road
Edinburgh EH9 1QS

www.birlinn.co.uk

ISBN 978 1 84158 565 9

British Library Cataloguing-in-Publication Data
A catalogue record for this book is available from the British Library

Typeset by Waverley Typesetters, Fakenham
Printed and bound by MPG Books Ltd, Bodmin

To Dorothea,
to celebrate 40 years together in 2009

Contents

Plates, Figures and Tables

Plates

Figures

Tables

Acknowledgements

Writing this book would have been much more difficult without access to the documents, objects and oral resources of Comann Eachdraidh Lios Mòr (The Lismore Historical Society). I am grateful to the founders and directors (Donald Black, Margaret MacDonald, Cathie Carmichael, Duncan Livingstone, John Livingstone, Archie MacColl, Archie MacGillivray, Duncan MacGregor, Sandy MacLean, Stuart Ross, Hubert Saldana and Mairi Smith) for their support. It is a pleasure to thank Donald Black, in particular, for his patient and enthusiastic answers to my many questions, and for his detailed advice on the chapters on more recent history.

In covering such a wide period of prehistory and history, I needed the help of experts. I am grateful that, in the course of very busy lives, they were able to give that help so willingly. Dr Fraser Hunter of the National Museum of Scotland advised on prehistory and gave me the opportunity to handle the Lismore armlet. Dr Susan Ramsay of the Department of Archaeology, University of Glasgow, provided not only the results of the preliminary archaeobotanical work on Lismore but also helpful interpretation. Over many conversations, Catherine Gillies explained the importance of the MacDougall dynasty, and correspondence with Dennis Turner clarified details about their castles. Alastair Campbell of Airds guided me through the historical sources for Clan Campbell, and Professor Jane Dawson of the Department of Theology, University of Edinburgh, was my guide not only to the Glenorchy branch but also to the course of the Reformation in Argyll. I am particularly grateful for her careful reading of the relevant parts of the book.

Dr Donald McWhannel gave helpful advice on the traditions of boat building in Argyll, and Drs Colin and Paula Martin were invaluable sources of information on the coast in general and lime kilns in particular. At a very busy time in her life, Paula found the time to provide invaluable editorial advice on the whole book. Towards the end of the project, Ronnie Black gave me much-needed encouragement, and greatly enhanced my understanding of the history of Gaeldom.

While writing the book I was continually aware of my debt to those who, over recent decades, have explored little-understood aspects of the history of the West Highlands and Islands. Their work is cited at the end of each chapter. I would also like to acknowledge the courteous help of staff at the National Archives of Scotland, the National Library of Scotland and the Central Library in Edinburgh.

Many people on the island have supported me through the project. My thanks to: Chris and Margaret Small for countless kindnesses; Margaret Black and Jennifer Baker, my co-curators at the Lismore Museum, for their wealth of information and help in many ways; Laura Gloag for her extensive knowledge of, and enthusiasm for, genealogy; John Raymond for excellent photographs (cover and Plates 2, 9–13, 14b); Stephen Green for keeping my computer up to scratch; Valerie and Alastair Livingstone for access to their letter archive; Cait McCulloch for her early support; and David and Catriona White, who impelled me to start the book and who have provided welcome challenges as well as encouragement.

Nevertheless, any errors of fact or judgement, transcription or interpretation must be my responsibility alone.

I would add a special thank-you to my editor, Andrew Simmons, whose quiet diplomacy has been essential to the publication of this book. As always, nothing would have been done without the patience and support of my wife, Dorothea.

Park, Lismore
August 2008

Note: The spelling of place names generally follows the lead given by Donald Black in *A Tale or Two from Lismore*. In spelling surnames (particularly Mc/Mac and Livingston/e) I have generally used the version in the relevant documents, and Mac and Livingstone for more modern names, but there is, inevitably, some inconsistency.

Introduction

Visitors to the Isle of Lismore ask so many questions. Why is the island so green, even in winter? Why are there no people in the south-east of the island? Why is there no centre of population with church, school and shop? Why are there two medieval castles on such a small island? What happened to the lime industry? When they get to know Lismore better they ask deeper questions, such as how the continuity of Gaelic was maintained on Lismore when it died out in so many small communities.

On their way to the island museum and café, they stop to look at what looks like a simple harled parish church, but this is what remains of the choir of the medieval cathedral of Argyll, turned back to front in a Victorian renovation. Inside they can find not only original architectural details of the cathedral but also monumental sculpture that is unique in Scotland. There are a few traces on the site of a much earlier Christian foundation – the Celtic monastery of Moluag, a contemporary of Columba; his blackthorn staff, 1,400 years old, is preserved by the Livingstone family nearby at Bachuil. Moluag came here because it was already an ancient centre of religion and authority. From near the church, the visitor can see the Iron Age broch at Tirfuir and two Bronze Age cairns, one at least associated with fire worship. A cup-marked stone lies at the highest point of the graveyard.

The aim of this book is to provide some answers to these questions, to describe and interpret the many prehistoric and historic sites and monuments on the island and to place them in the context of what was happening elsewhere in the British Isles and northern Europe. Because it covers the whole story from the earliest people, it can only sketch out each period, and there is ample room, and a real need, for more detailed studies. It would be good to know more about the MacDougalls (builders of the castles at Achinduin and Coeffin, and the cathedral), and the bishopric of Argyll, and there are opportunities for exploring life on the island from 1500 onwards from the extensive Argyll and Glenorchy archives. The most pressing need is for a history of the role of the island in fostering the Gaelic language, tracing the thread from the *Book of the Dean of Lismore*, through the many contributions of island ministers to the translation of the Bible and liturgy, and the collaboration between Rev. Donald McNicol and Duncan Ban McIntyre, to the astonishing collection of oral traditions by Alexander Carmichael. Indeed the thread did not end there: the daughter of Captain Eoghan Anderson published *Measan Millis as an Lios*, a collection of his Gaelic songs, in 1925, and the tradition of putting Gaelic words to music was carried well into the twentieth century by the MacDonald bards (Chapter 11).

The Land

From the top of Cnoc Aingeal, the fire cairn of Lismore, you look northwards into the jaws of an Earth movement of unimaginable scale and age. Three blocks of crust, wandering over the surface of the planet, collided with such force that their edges crumpled upwards into mountains of Himalayan proportions. After many millions of years of erosion, only their roots survive as the modest mountains of the Scottish Highlands, Norway, Greenland and the Appalachians. But the collision had other important consequences for the area: as is happening today in California, and on the coast of Sumatra, the intense mechanical stresses caused the rocks to tear, or fault, and slip sideways in huge slabs. As a result of the greatest of these tears, the Great Glen Fault, the western rocks moved southwards in relation to the eastern rocks, in a long series of violent movements, so that the matching geologies of Strontian and Foyers finally ended up 65 miles apart. Even now, 400–500 million years later, aftershocks of these events are still being recorded as earthquakes in the Great Glen, the most recent in October 2008 near Glenfinnan.

This crumpling, squeezing, twisting and heating somehow combined to lift up, into the middle of the Fault, a slice of ancient limestone that eventually would form Lismore, Shuna and many of the small islands and skerries. These rocks had been laid down in cold clear water at the South Pole, in the earliest days of life on Earth, before the appearance of forms that would give easily recognised fossils. Their rough handling in the crust caused the original layers to be contorted into complex curves, turned on end or completely overturned, and mixed at high temperatures with dark mudstones (slates and shales) to give the familiar hard

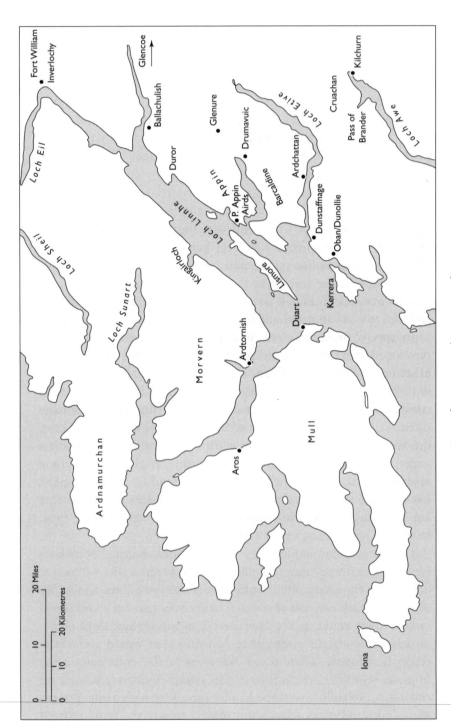

FIGURE 1.1 Map of Lismore and its surrounding areas.

grey marbly rock (Plate 1a). In places the limestone was injected with veins of pure white quartz, while the high iron content of the original sediments is shown by crystals of pyrites, and red and orange staining of some cleaved surfaces. Later, the opening of the Atlantic Ocean brought different stresses. The crust was stretched this time, and it failed again, leaving wide cracks which, across much of Scotland, were filled with molten rock from volcanoes in the west. The Lismore cracks were infiltrated, under pressure and high temperatures, from great calderas of lava in Mull and Ardnamurchan. In some cases, the intruded rock proved to be more resistant than the limestone, giving the prominent natural dykes in the south of the island that look from the distance to be man-made walls (Plate 1b); elsewhere the rapid erosion of the new rock produced steep gulleys between limestone cliffs, running down to the sea.

This was not the end of the violence done to the Lismore rocks. A series of ice ages, which did not finish until around 10,000 years ago, cleared away any soils and vegetation that might have developed, effectively sterilising the area. At the height of the glaciation of Scotland, there was an ice cap on Rannoch Moor with glaciers moving outwards in all directions, grinding exposed rocks, deepening any existing valleys, and moving great quantities of rock debris on, in and below the ice. Erratic boulders of Etive granite, stranded high up on top of the limestone on Lismore (Plate 1c), show that the ice was flowing from the east, but it was turned towards the south-west by a glacier moving down the Great Glen, determining the orientation of the island glens and lochs. At the end of thousands of years of gouging and grinding, the ice began to retreat around 15,000 to 18,000 years ago, dumping on the polished surface a jumbled layer of mixed rock material of all sizes from clay, through sand and cobbles, to boulders.

Although the glaciers had started to retreat, it would be thousands of years before man made his appearance on the scene. The great weight of ice on the west of Scotland had actually pushed the crust downwards so that when the melting released vast quantities of water Lismore was almost completely inundated by the sea. Over many centuries the land rebounded slowly and the sea level on the island fell, but, from around 8,500 years ago, the process stalled, and the level remained around 10m above the present for as much as 3,000 years, giving time for the sea to carve prominent raised beaches, cliffs and caves (Plate 1d). After this, the rise of the land resumed to the present stable level, but there are areas of Scandinavia, freed of ice much later than Scotland, where the land is still rising at a measurable rate each year.

The unique limestone geology of Lismore and the surrounding islands has played a central part in making the story of the land and people quite different from that of other parts of Argyll and the West Highlands and Islands. Throughout historical times, and probably much earlier, farmers realised that there was something special about the soils of Lismore; the ring of duns, forts and brochs round the coast of the island looks suspiciously like a set of defences against Iron Age neighbours casting covetous eyes on their grain stores and fat cattle.

The soils of the north and west of Scotland are generally infertile because most of their starting materials – schists, quartzites and granites – are poor in nutrients, particularly calcium, and the climate is wet. Plants need to absorb calcium for healthy growth but lime is also important in counteracting the tendency for all soils to become more acidic as the drainage of water carries away soluble materials. Wet acid soils are difficult to cultivate: the acidity limits the range and yield of crops that can thrive and the biological activity of the soil is low, severely reducing the amount of nitrogen available from natural fixation by legumes such as clover, and soil bacteria. Traditionally, the communities of the West Highlands grew grain where they could, on favourable patches of well-drained soil, heavily manured with dung and seaware. But they relied for their income on rearing small black cattle, mostly on unimproved grassland, for sale to drovers who walked them south in great numbers to the annual sales at Crieff and Falkirk. They were in the business of exporting protein but two of the crucial inputs (plant nitrogen to build muscle and calcium to build bone) were severely limited by soil acidity. The great demand for Highland cattle, particularly after the Union of the Parliaments in 1707, was based on their hardiness and the quality of the meat.

The hard and slowly dissolving Lismore limestone did not contribute much mass to the island soils. Most of the raw material, from clay to boulders, was gathered by the ice from the lime-poor rocks to the east and north of the island, but since most of the soils are quite shallow, plant roots can grow down to the slowly dissolving rock and carry calcium upwards for eventual return to the soil surface in leaf litter. This circulation was particularly effective under the natural vegetation of hazel, elm, oak and ash, with little plant material taken away. Even after many centuries, with little or no agricultural lime added, some of the island soils under semi-natural grassland are still only slightly acidic, in the ideal range for productivity. The contrast with the rest of Argyll was at its most extreme at the time of the First Statistical Account in the 1790s, when the parish minister, Donald McNicol, reported that the Lismore tenants paid their rents in the form of grain and meal, rather than from raising livestock. Apart from shallow rocky and low-lying boggy areas, almost the whole of Lismore was devoted to raising bere barley and oats, with cattle and sheep banished beyond the head dyke or shipped to outlying islands during the growing season. The contrast is much less marked now, with grazing and silage production dominating as elsewhere in Argyll, but low light in winter reveals traces of former cultivation ridges everywhere on the island, even in the most unexpected, isolated places (Plate 2). Great piles of stone testify to the work done to clear the soil for the spade and plough.

The relative fertility of Lismore (Lios Mòr, 'the great garden') has made it an object of desire since the introduction of agriculture; the following chapters explore the conflicts for possession with invading Vikings and among the leading families in Argyll until it was absorbed into the Campbell (Argyll and Glenorchy) empire. Its fertility also had important implications for the ordinary people of the islands, for example in terms of human population growth, land tenure, and the high rents exacted by landowners.

Fertility brought one serious, chronic problem for the islanders. Even on Barr Mòr, the highest point, the limestone outcrops are interspersed with relatively fertile and well-drained soil, supporting grassland rather than heather and mosses, the raw materials for the development of peat. With much of the tree and scrub cover disappearing as more and more of the island was cropped or grazed, the supply of fuel for cooking and heating ran out. Before the advent of the coal boat, much of the time in the summer was spent in small open boats, transporting peat from the mainland or exploiting the woods of Kingairloch. These were arduous and hazardous enterprises. The alternative to the very limited peat banks was the organic-rich mud accumulating round the lochs, which islanders moulded into a far from satisfactory fuel with little fibre to bind the blocks. When the Rev. Dr John Walker visited in 1771 he found that handling and burning this greasy material in cottages with central hearths caused the islanders to have unique sallow complexions, quite different to those of the neighbouring natives of Mull.

Throughout history, seafarers have been very wary of the inhospitable rock-bound coast of the island and its outlying rocks, but the high incidence of wrecks round its coast was finally brought to an end when Robert Stevenson built the lighthouse on Eilean Musdile in 1833, followed by a range of other smaller lights and beacons. Small boats can be pulled up safely on pebbly beaches in various places and there is a sheltered rocky inlet at Sailean, but the geology of the island dictates where bigger boats can lie at anchor or be hauled out for maintenance. Only where the glaciers cut down into softer slates in the north-west can bigger boats find secure shelter; even here, the entry to the anchorage is guarded by hidden skerries and the bays are open to winds from the north. When, in the nineteenth century, the islanders exploited limestone as a valuable resource for export, the uniquely (for Lismore) muddy and sheltered Port Ramsay (Plate 3) was the principal harbour of the island, with several resident owners and masters of sailing smacks trading in coal and lime.

To a certain extent the geology of the island also dominated the pattern of settlement through the availability of drinking water. As in most limestone landscapes, the underlying rock is generally porous. Rainwater passing through the soil tends to be channelled into subterranean voids, and there are few sizeable burns. Many of the older farming townships were associated with ancient wells; where burns do occur, such as those draining the three freshwater lochs, they were harnessed for milling. Finally, where the rock cleaved naturally, it provided a suitable material for dry-stone building, at the domestic level, but also in grander and more complicated structures such as the Tirfuir broch, whose unmortared double walls may originally have risen to more than 10m (see cover illustration).

Bibliography

Fortey, R. (2004) *The Earth: An Intimate History*. London: HarperCollins.

Hickman, A.H. (1975) 'The stratigraphy of late Precambrian metasediments between Glen Roy and Lismore.' *Scottish Journal of Geology* 11: 117–42 (includes a geological map of Lismore).

McKay, M.M. (ed.) (1980) *The Rev. Dr John Walker's Report on the Hebrides of 1764 and 1771*. Edinburgh: John Donald.

Whittow, J.B. (1977) *Geology and Scenery in Scotland*. London: Penguin.

The First People

Around 10,000 years ago, the ice finally disappeared, and northern Europe experienced many centuries of weather that was warmer than today. The young soils, not yet stripped of nutrients, were enriched with nitrogen by the first colonising plants, preparing the way for the early arrival of birch and hazel woodland, with willows in wetter areas. On Lismore, the pioneer woodland was succeeded on deeper soils predominantly by elm forest with oak, and alder slowly invaded the island wetlands. There was ample cover for the animals that were able to cross the Linn of Lorn, including brown bear, wolf, lynx, red deer, wild boar and smaller game. There was an abundance of fish in the sea and shellfish on the shore.

The people who moved into Scotland from around 7,000 to 8,000 years ago knew what they were doing. They were not driven by hunger or pressure of population, and their outdoor life was favoured by a warm dry climate. Hunting further and further into the new lands, they found opportunities for more settled living, and brought their families north and west. With thousands of years of experience of making their living near the edge of the ice, they had the skills, social structures and the mental flexibility to exploit the resources of the new wilderness. By dugout canoe or skin coracle, they spread out along the coast and the inner isles, moving in small family groups, living off the seasonal abundance in food (fish, shellfish, game, hazelnuts, berries). They had a toolkit that included fishing nets, hunting weapons, tools of stone and wood, a range of raw materials including skins, fibres, bone, antler and birch bark, and fire for cooking, heating, hunting and protection.

The fact that they soon reached more isolated islands such as Rum shows that they would have had no difficulty in crossing to Lismore but, because Mesolithic folk travelled light, possessing only what they could carry, they have left few traces on the island. Where caves have been reused many times throughout history, and the land intensively cultivated for hundreds of years, it is difficult to find the scattered fragments of stone and traces of shelters of wood and skin that would confirm their presence over 3,000 or 4,000 years. There are full accounts of archaeological excavations nearby (caves in Oban, enormous piles of shells and bones on Oronsay, other finds in Jura and Ulva), but the evidence for Lismore rests on largely undocumented digging in caves and shelters on Eilean Dubh, Eilean na Cloiche and Shuna. It was once thought that Mesolithic people were very thin on the ground in Scotland, but intensive surveys of Jura, Islay and Colonsay and the shorelines around Skye, looking for their characteristic microlithic tools of flint and other workable stone, have revealed that the resources along much of the coast were exploited at times during this long period of prehistory. It is likely that a similar search for suitable sites at the 10m shoreline on Lismore (running fresh water, caves, practical access to the shore and sea, shelter from prevailing winds), for example at Sailean and Port Ramsay, would provide similar evidence of long occupation. With a total population in Scotland probably numbering thousands rather than tens of thousands, it seems unlikely that Mesolithic folk would have had much impact on their environment, other than localised extinction of game species. However, charcoal in peat cores taken near Balnagowan Loch show that there was very early firing of the island vegetation, possibly by Mesolithic man.

More intensive population of the mainland and islands began from around 6,000 years ago with the coming of agriculture and more permanent settlements. In her dramatic recreation of the arrival of early farmers in Argyll, Marion Campbell draws on the fact that, worldwide and even until quite recently in some areas, hunter-gatherers and cultivators co-existed and possibly even cooperated, as long as their activities were not in conflict. The earliest Neolithic people on the western seaboard took their harvests from the sea and forest, as well as from farmed land, gradually relying more and more on crops (barley and primitive forms of wheat) and livestock, as the land was cleared. Archaeological excavation of an early site on Islay found that people were keeping sheep and collecting hazelnuts from the wild, and there is an unbroken hunter-gatherer approach to food from the sea to this day. Hunting and gathering on land would have become progressively more marginal as agriculture expanded.

Unlike in Orkney, where they built durable homes in stone, Neolithic folk in Argyll used earth, wood and other perishable materials. As a result, there are few traces of their presence on Lismore, where the surface of the land was thoroughly disturbed by the plough in later times. The first farmers turned to stone only to accommodate their dead. Chambered cairns for burials, the first concrete evidence of organised ritual and religion, are common throughout southern Argyll and Arran but uncommon north of Kilmartin. Perhaps there were fewer people of sufficient status to justify, or command, the amount of work involved. On a terrace of naturally well-drained land above Kilcheran Loch on Lismore, near the deserted settlement of Cloichlea, lie four great stones that appear, at first sight, to be the wreckage of a Neolithic burial chamber, with the capstone thrown aside (Plate 4). In fact, according to oral tradition, this was a great erratic (Cloich Liath – the grey stone) that was blown up in the nineteenth century, but not cleared from the field because of uneasy feelings about its value. The ritual importance of the original stone in the Neolithic period is confirmed by a series of simple cup marks on one of the fragments. There is a larger cup mark, known as the baptismal stone, in the kirkyard; another cup-marked stone was recovered during excavation at Tirfuir Broch, and it is likely that there are many more to be discovered. Two polished ceremonial axe heads of Appin stone (Plate 5a), dating from around 3,500 BC, have been found in different parts of the island, but there is also definite evidence of the activities of the first farmers in the peat cores taken at Balnagowan and Fiart lochs. The steep decline in tree pollen and the rise of grasses and cereals shows that settlers were making serious inroads into the woodland and scrub cover of the island by fire and axe.

Studies of the genetics of the people living in the British Isles have demonstrated that, even today, in spite of increasing mobility, those in the west and north of England, Wales and Scotland generally belong to the same population, originating with the first farmers, or possibly even earlier settlers. The early Irish chroniclers, writing first around the sixth century AD, referred to the main population of Ireland and the native tribes of what would be northern Scotland jointly as the Cruithne. This name has caused a great deal of controversy among prehistorians, including the unlikely theory that the original people of Ireland were Picts. In reality, Cruithne may simply be the early Gaelic form of 'Briton', referring to the common origin of the peoples.

Looking more widely, it appears that the people of the Atlantic fringe, from Spain to Scotland, have been there from the beginning, and that the major changes in technology, language and ritual that occurred over many centuries arrived by cultural diffusion, probably assisted by small-scale immigration (for example, of potters, metal workers and stone carvers). Much later there were major intrusions of other groups (Germanic people/ Angles and Saxons in the east up to the Firth of Forth in Scotland; Scandinavians in the Danelaw of England and in the Northern Isles and Outer Hebrides in Scotland) but the people who moved from Northern Ireland into the West Highlands and Islands belonged to the same foundation stock. It is, however, important to be aware of the contributions of individuals, such as Somerled, from elsewhere (Chapter 5).

In the prehistory of the British Isles, therefore, change occurred mainly through the exchange of ideas, of necessities and luxuries, of tools, and of handcrafted goods. In Argyll, Neolithic people made their own fairly crude fired-clay containers but imported superior pottery. They traded for stone suitable for knapping into tools from Arran, Ireland and the Lake District, and items from further afield turn up in excavations. The early farmers in Lismore should, therefore, not be seen as an isolated group but as part of a continuous cultural highway (really a seaway) from the Aegean and Mediterranean via Spain, France and Ireland, to the west of Britain. Movement along the coast could be faster and safer than through the forested land, and less demanding than crossing the North Sea, which had filled to nearly its present area by 7,000 years ago. Lismore may well have played an important role as a branch point in this seaway, leading the way to the east coast of Scotland by the Great Glen. The importance of the movement and development of ideas during the Neolithic period can be seen in the architectural achievements at Callanish in Lewis, and in Orkney (the Ring of Brodgar and Maes Howe), constructed around 5,000 years ago.

By around 4,500 years ago, metal working had become established in the British Isles, based mainly on copper from North Wales and tin from the mines in Cornwall that supplied most of Europe. Although there is no evidence of metal working in Argyll at this time, over the following centuries an indigenous and creative industry developed elsewhere in Scotland, and both imported and more local bronze weapons and body ornaments begin to appear in increasing numbers. Around the same time there were very obvious changes in the way that the dead were treated and in the monuments set up as memorials or for other ritual purposes. The Bronze Age, which lasted for nearly 2,000 years in Britain, left some very obvious marks on Lismore.

Neolithic chambered cairns were opened up and reused for several burials but, some time before the arrival of the use of metal, came the idea of burying single bodies (presumably of an elite minority only) intact in a crouched position within a box of stone slabs (a cist), accompanied by a pottery vessel. Opinion is divided over whether the vessel held food and drink for the last journey. In later centuries, the body was incinerated before burial. Characteristic beakers with imprints of cords and food vessels of various shapes similar to those found in Ireland have been recovered from different sites in Argyll, but the two surviving examples of intact cists (without capstones) on the island, high up on Barr Mòr and Aon Garbh, were long ago robbed of their contents. A bronze-socketed axe from nearby on Barr Mòr (Plate 5b) is the only surviving Bronze Age find from the island. Three more broken cists have been identified at the cairn to the west of Kilcheran Loch (Druim an Uinnsinn), and in 1790 a burial of bones and ashes associated with a pottery vessel was uncovered near the Cnoc Aingeal cairn, but details of the site and the contents have been lost.

These five cists were not placed randomly in the landscape. They fall on the straight line of cairns which runs from the crest of the south of the island on Aon Garbh, above the deserted township of Achanard, to the summit of Barr Mòr, and to the north and west of Kilcheran Loch. Extending this line across the island shows that the standing stone on Eilean Musdile (lost during the building of the lighthouse) to the south, and the two great cairns (Cnoc Aingeal and Carn Mòr) at Clachan nearer the north end (Plate 7a), are also part of the Bronze Age alignment, nearly 10 miles long (Figure 2.1). Some, at least, of the cairns are kerbed and date from the later Bronze Age, and the only contemporary monuments on Lismore that are not on the alignment are three more cairns at Baligrundle. All have been robbed to some extent for dyke building, none has been systematically excavated to find out whether it contains a burial, and it is likely that others have

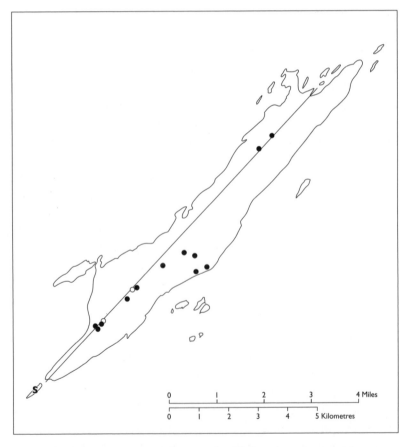

FIGURE 2.1   Bronze Age monuments. The filled circles are cairns, the empty circles separate cists and S indicates the position of the standing stone on Eilean Musdile, lost during the building of the lighthouse.

been completely removed in more intensively farmed areas. Similar linear arrangements of monuments are found elsewhere in Lorn (Kilmore and Benderloch) and, most spectacularly, at Kilmartin, where the whole landscape is thought to have had a religious or ritual significance.

It is almost impossible to interpret the religious concepts of pre-literate cultures, but there are important clues from elsewhere in northern Europe. For example, inscribed bronze razors from this period found in Denmark illustrate the importance of the cult of the sun and its daily passage across the sky. Stylised carvings show the sun pulled out of the sea to the east in the morning by a fish, transferred from its boat to a chariot, and drawn across the noon sky by a horse. (The gilded Trundholm Sun Chariot drawn by a bronze horse is possibly the most spectacular object in the prehistoric section of the Danish National Museum.) Later in the afternoon, the sun, returned to its boat, is drawn down to the underworld, and through the underworld from west back to east by a snake. In this mythology, the sun relies on four helpers: boat, fish, horse and snake. It is striking that, around the same period in Egypt, before the building of the main pyramids, the cult of Atum, the god of creation and the sun, involved the circulation of the sun in a boat and his struggle with the serpent in the underworld to move from west to east in the hours of darkness. In Greek Bronze Age mythology, Apollo was the god of light, who favoured high places. This all helps in understanding the Lismore alignment. The cairns are on the highest parts of the island, affording a clear perspective of the sky and the passage of the sun from east to west. Those buried in the cists were placed as near as possible to the sky, with breathtaking views on all sides, from Ben Nevis to Cruachan to Mull (Plate 1b).

As at Kilmartin, the direction of the alignment may have astronomical significance, or it may simply have been dictated by the lie of the land. What seems to be clear, however, is that the north end, around Clachan, had a particular significance in terms of ritual and power which has persisted into the modern world. Moluag chose his main monastic site to be in the shadow of Carn Mòr and not far from the pagan fire cairn, Cnoc Aingeal; it was the site chosen for the cathedral of Argyll; and it has played subsequent roles in terms of justice, execution and sanctuary over the centuries. Today it is the site of the parish church and the sole burial ground on the island.

Again, as at Kilmartin, there is little archaeological evidence on Lismore of everyday life, homes and farming during the Bronze Age, although there has not been a systematic search for hut circles on the island. The first clear signs of domestic life do not appear until later, with the appearance of Iron Age roundhouses, probably fortified family farms (Chapter 3). The assemblage of Bronze Age monuments on the island and their interrelationships are important for the understanding of the period in Scotland. It is regrettable that there has been so little systematic field work in the area.

Bibliography

Butter, R. (1999) *Kilmartin: An Introduction and Guide*. Kilmartin House Trust.

Campbell, M. (2001) *Argyll: The Enduring Heartland*. Colonsay: House of Lochar.

Ramsay, S. and Housley, R. (2007) 'Island of Lismore. Preliminary Pollen Analysis: An Environmental Archaeology Study, Project 2195.' Report to Historic Scotland.

Ritchie, G. (ed.) (1997) *The Archaeology of Argyll*. Edinburgh: Edinburgh University Press.

'Scotland's First Settlers' at http://www.oisf.org.uk/sfs/sfs_2002.htm.

Wickham-Jones, C.R. (2003) *Scotland's First Settlers*. London: Batsford.

3

3℣

Iron Age Celts

Changes in the availability and quality of metal tools and weapons were central to the development of early societies, but the advance of technology was not a matter of steady progress. Prehistoric communities experienced many setbacks. For example, in some areas, the change from hunter-gathering to farming resulted in a decline in the quality of the diet and in the health of individuals but an increase in the number that could be fed. In a similar way, the fact that the properties of the iron produced in Iron Age Europe were inferior to those of the bronze indicates that the change to widespread use of iron happened for reasons other than technological advance. Nevertheless, it did have an important impact in placing lower-grade metal tools and weapons in the hands of many more people.

Pure copper is a soft metal, of little use to early man other than in jewellery or other ornaments, but alloying it with 5 per cent of tin and small proportions of other elements, particularly arsenic, to give bronze, transformed its properties. Copper ores and native copper metal are fairly widespread throughout the world, including small ore bodies in Argyll, but the only significant source of tin in prehistoric Europe was in Cornwall. Elsewhere there was mining of tin in Mesopotamia (where bronze metallurgy is thought to have begun) and Thailand. There were many advantages in the use of bronze for tools, containers, weapons, armour and ornaments: it is strong and hard, it is readily sharpened to a durable edge, it does not rust, and it can be smelted and cast at relatively low temperatures. However, the vulnerability of the trade in tin was probably the major factor in the switch to iron production.

Iron is common, making up 7 per cent of the Earth's crust, and it occurs in the form of iron oxide and other ores throughout the world, including the 'bog iron ores' formed in bogs and marshes in many parts of northern Europe, including Scotland. The basic technology of producing iron metal was similar to that for copper and tin (firing in small, clay furnaces with charcoal, driven by leather bellows, producing carbon monoxide, which reduced the metal oxide) but, because of the higher temperatures needed to melt iron (above 1,500°C), the product was in the form of a solid and impure 'bloom', which was malleable when hot and could be hammered into shape (i.e. blacksmith work). It was not until the introduction of early types of blast furnace in the medieval period that Europeans were able to pour purer liquid metal for casting, and to manufacture more useful and durable steels (alloys of iron and carbon). Unlike bronze smelting, which remained a relatively specialised activity supported by a complex web of trading, once the procedure for smelting iron was mastered it could be carried out wherever there were supplies of charcoal and iron ore, and these were plentiful in Scotland. Recent excavations at Culduthel, near Inverness, have revealed the first major Iron Age bloomery to be found in Scotland.

Iron products were not as hard as bronze and they deteriorated by rusting, but they came to predominate for everyday use because of the security of supplies and lower costs. Nevertheless, bronze objects were still greatly prized: most of the surviving finely-worked metal artefacts (daggers, swords, helmets, shields, brooches) from the workshops of the Celtic Iron Age Hallstatt (c. 1200–450 BC) and La Tène (c. 450–50 BC) cultures in Central Europe are in durable bronze, silver or gold, and Roman writers in the later centuries of the Iron Age describe Gaulish warriors as wearing bronze helmets. The iron objects have generally rusted away. The technical and artistic standards of bronze working in Scotland continued to develop in the Iron Age, with the inclusion of lead to reduce the temperature for casting and the production of characteristic armlets and bracelets, some of which were further decorated with enamel work.

The single most important archaeological find from Lismore is the impressive bronze armlet found by chance at Newfield near Achnacroish in 1991 (Plate 6). It was cast in the early centuries of the Christian era from recycled Roman metal with a high zinc content by craftsmen in the north-east of Scotland. Worn by men in pairs, one on each upper arm, these armlets would have been a sign of wealth and power, but the Lismore armlet is the smallest known example, presumably worn by the son of a leading family (there is a contemporary range of bracelets for women). The characteristic 'trumpet' motif, a direct development of La Tène decoration, appears on all of the 30 surviving armlets, 28 found on the east coast of Scotland and one at Newry in Northern Ireland. This distribution underlines the role of Lismore as a crossing point on the trade routes along the west coast and through the Great Glen, although it has also been suggested that the Lismore find could have arisen out of the fostering of a son of an east-coast ruling family.

The insecurity of the world at the start of the Iron Age not only disrupted trade but probably also increased the demand for weapons. Around 800 BC there was an abrupt change in climate in north-west Europe from warm continental to cooler and wetter (oceanic or Atlantic) conditions. This led to a rise in the water table along the coast, with the archaeological record showing the abandonment of settlements in northern Europe and widespread expansion of marshes and bogs. The effects were particularly marked in Scotland, with the advance of blanket bog over much of the uplands, and this tipped the balance of conditions for farming: areas on the west coast that had been marginal for growing grain went out of production. At a time when the population was rising, the supply of arable land was decreasing. Later in the Iron Age, the expansion of the Roman Empire also increased the instability at its fringes. After the initial invasion of Britain in AD 43, the Roman legions had reached the Forth–Clyde line by AD 78 and were penetrating deeply into the territory of the northern tribes.

These developments help to explain the unusual density and distribution of Iron Age monuments on Lismore. In contrast to the linear arrangement of Bronze Age cairns and cists high up on the ridge, the Iron Age structures (small forts and 'Atlantic roundhouses' – duns and brochs, most probably constructed in the centuries from 400 BC to AD 200) are nearly all at the coast and predominantly on the east side (Figure 3.1). The most common roundhouses, the duns, were built on naturally defensible sites,

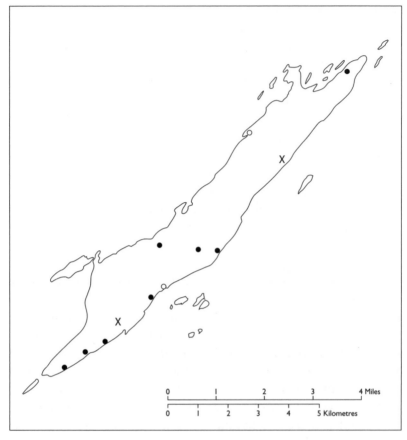

Figure 3.1   Iron Age monuments. The filled circles are duns, the
empty circles forts and the crosses brochs.

partly protected by sea cliffs and steep slopes. The most dramatic
is the furthest south, Dun Chrubain (Plate 7b), which commands
the approach by sea from the south and east. Its building platform,
reached by a scramble over steep rocks, is bounded by a vertical
fall of nearly 8m to the north. Dun Mòr, inland at Baligrundle, is
protected by a cliff to the north and a deep natural ditch to the
south. It is likely that there was also a dun at Achinduin.

The duns are circular or oval, of varying internal diameter: less
than 10m (Park and Kilcheran); around 15m (Chrubain and Sean);
or greater than 20m (Sloc a'Bhrighide, Fiart, Mòr and Cuilein).
Their walls, generally robbed of stone to near ground level, vary

in thickness from 3m to 5m. They were, presumably, dry-stone towers with timber or thatched roofing, but it is not possible to estimate their original height. Some of the duns with thicker walls may, in fact, have been brochs, with more complex architecture. The sites of Park Dun and Sean Dun have been excavated recently without yielding clues to the use of the buildings, but study of duns elsewhere in Argyll suggests that the internal space was divided into living accommodation by wooden partitions. A late Iron Age rotary 'bun' quern for milling grain was found at Park.

The two forts at Coeffin and Kilcheran are more extensive (oval, 120m × 40m and 80m × 30m), and more irregular. Their encircling walls, between 3m and 4m thick, were, presumably, defensive rather than an integral part of the accommodation, and little structure survives. It is likely that they are earlier than the duns, protecting communal settlements rather than individual farming families, and this is supported by traces of hut circles 8.5m in diameter within the Kilcheran fort.

It is now generally accepted that duns were fortified farmhouses, set in an area of good land, each occupied by a single, fairly high-ranking family. The clearest example of this arrangement is Park Dun, placed within an ancient enclosure of around 4 acres that has probably been farmed since prehistory. The possession and defence of such areas of well-drained, non-acidic and productive soils had become crucially important with the change in climate, and the instability caused by Roman pressure to the south. The threat presumably came from the more populated eastern mainland rather than from the west, and the clustering of duns towards the south of the island indicates a greater concentration of population, which continued until the depopulation of the nineteenth century (Chapter 10). Nevertheless, there are clear lines of sight from Park Dun to Tirfuir Broch to Sean Dun; from Dun Mòr to Tirfuir; and from Dun Cuilein in the west at Frackersaig to Coeffin and Achinduin and probably to Dun Mòr (when the dun walls were at full height) (Figure 3.1), showing the possibility of signalling and concerted action throughout the island in the event of an attack.

The finding of a Roman enamelled brooch (Plate 8a) in the foundation layer at Tirfuir Broch fixes the date of its construction within the first century AD. It may have been principally a statement of power and prestige, the seat of the most powerful family on the island. Even today, reduced from its original height (probably 10m or more), it is still a dominating presence from the Linn of Lorn. It is a classic broch structure, with a tapering outline skilfully built in dry stone, hollow walls 4.5m thick accommodating galleries and a stairway, and a defendable narrow entrance facing west-south-west. With an internal diameter of 12.2m at the base, it is smaller than some of the Lismore duns, but it is similar in style and scale to the large brochs in Orkney, Lewis and Wester Ross. The prominent shelf at around 2.5m above the ground level was presumably the support for a floor for the living quarters, with livestock below, but opinion varies about the roofing of broch accommodation. There are traces of protective walls across the ridge to the south-west and north-east. The surviving lower courses of another structure overlooking Loch Fiart indicate that it may also have been a broch.

As elsewhere in Argyll, there are no identifiable traces of burials or, indeed, of the living accommodation of the bulk of the population during the Iron Age (700 BC to AD 500), but there can be no doubt that there was a substantial population on the island in the early centuries AD. Very large teams of skilled masons and labourers would have been needed to build the broch and to achieve the almost Inca style of building of the foundations of Dun Chrubain, with huge, tightly fitting boulders (Plate 7b). Preliminary archaeological studies, including identification of pollen and other plant remains, indicate that by the Iron Age the island was almost entirely cleared of woodland (although clauses for the protection of trees in leases up to the eighteenth century show that small woods did persist). From the Bronze Age onwards, up to the peak of illicit distilling (Chapter 9), six-row barley (bere) was the major crop grown on Lismore, but the finding of many hazelnut shells shows that Iron Age people continued to collect food from the wild.

Celtic Lismore

At what point can we be justified in calling the people on Lismore Celtic – that is, speaking a Celtic language? There was no large-scale immigration of Celtic tribes from their heartland in Central Europe or from Gaul, but archaeology shows that their technological and artistic ideas had certainly penetrated as far as Ireland and the west of Scotland, through trade, exchange or copying, by the early centuries of the Iron Age. It is not possible to find out exactly when, how or why Celtic languages came to predominate in the British Isles in the apparent absence of coercion, but it is known from the development of the languages that the change had taken place before the start of the Christian era. Understanding something of this development is important in unravelling the early history of Lismore because the spread of Gaelic across what was to be Scotland was a major part of political and religious change.

Around 1000 BC, the 'proto-Celtic' language spoken by people across Europe from the North Sea to the Black Sea underwent a major split. One branch, Q-Celtic, appears to have developed in Iberia (Celtiberian) and its closest modern relations are Scots, Irish Gaelic and Manx (the Goidelic languages). Movement of the language from Spain to Ireland along the Atlantic seaway is consistent with an Irish tradition of the arrival of aristocratic warriors (the 'Milesians') from Galicia. P-Celtic, the now-extinct language of the Gauls, crossed the North Sea to dominate throughout Great Britain in the form of the Brythonic languages (Welsh, Cumbric, Cornish), and it is generally accepted that the language of the tribes beyond the Forth–Clyde line (known from around AD 300 as Picts) was also P-Celtic, although it did not develop as a written language.

As the curtain of history rises on the early centuries of the Christian era, the evolving scene, described by writers in Latin and bards in the Irish hero tales, shows the British Isles to be occupied by loose groupings of agrarian tribes with hierarchies of kings, warriors, priests (druids), lawyers, bards, musicians and celebrity smiths. Their lives are portrayed as a series of raids and feuds, sporting competitions, storytelling and feasts, but the tales have little to say about the ordinary folk. A major difficulty in understanding this society, and how the politics of the future Ireland and Scotland developed, lies in the idea that there could have been a sharp linguistic divide across the North Channel: two groups, the Goidelic-speaking Irish, and the P-Celtic-speaking tribes on the eastern side (in modern Argyll, including Lismore, and Galloway), quite distinct, possibly mutually incomprehensible, but living within sight of each other. In an age when travel by sea was easier than by land, there must have been a continuous exchange of people (raiders, asylum seekers, traders, travelling smiths, potters and bards) and goods, in peace and war, culminating eventually in the establishment of the joint kingdom of Dalriada (Chapter 4). It is hardly necessary to propose that some of the Irish spoke a P-Celtic language to explain, as we shall see in the next chapter, why Columba (from Derry) is said to have needed an interpreter to communicate with the Picts to the east of Drumalban, the watershed of Scotland, whereas Moluag (from Bangor) did not. It is more likely that many people, including Moluag, were bilingual.

The Ulster Cycle of hero tales, composed around 2,000 years ago and transmitted orally for several hundred years before being written down by the monks, illustrates this ease of passage. Cuchulainn, the Hound of Ulster, is sent to Skye to learn the most advanced fighting skills from the woman warrior Scathach; the sons of Usnach, fleeing overseas as the protectors of Deirdre of the Sorrows, seek service with the 'King of Scotland', spending years of idyllic peace in Glen Etive in Argyll. More important for Lismore is the Finn Cycle, dating from around AD 300. Finn mac Cumhaill (known in Scotland as Fingal) and his fighting band, the Fianna or Feinne, were paid to serve Cormac the High King of Ireland from November to May, acting as a form of militia, protecting the country against invasion. Their 'summer holidays' were spent hunting and feasting in different parts of Ireland and 'Scotland'. At the north end of Lismore, there are several ancient place names, in Gaelic, referring to Finn, the Fianna, and their hunting exploits:

> Finncnockan/Fianna-Chnocan – the hillock of Finn or the Fianna
>
> Eilean Loch Osgair – the island in Loch Oscair (Oscair the grandson of Finn)
>
> Sliabh nam Ban Fiann – the slope of the Fingalian women (where they sat watching them hunting)
>
> Port nam Mòrlaoch – Port of the Great Heroes
>
> Làrach Taigh nam Fiana – the place of the Fingalians' house

These hero tales were common currency in the Celtic world of western Britain and Ireland from the late Iron Age onwards. The high incidence of Fingalian names on Lismore does not mean that the events recorded in the surviving fragments of these hero poems actually happened on the island. What it does suggest is that there was a strong bardic tradition, with local storytellers associating the hero tales with likely places in the landscape.

Whether or not the Finn Cycle was recited by bards in the roundhouses on Lismore in P-Celtic before Gaelic became the dominant language, the hero tales remained an important part of the cultural scene in the West Highlands well into medieval times. As shown by the *Book of the Dean of Lismore* (Chapter 8), versions had been collected and committed to writing in Scots Gaelic by the sixteenth century. Two centuries later, James McPherson claimed to have tapped into authentic oral and written sources in the Highlands and Islands for his *Poems of Ossian* (Fingal's son), including stories of Fingal hunting with the Fianna on Morvern. After Dr Johnson had publicly ridiculed Ossian, the minister of Lismore, Donald McNicol (1735–1802), published a strong defence of McPherson, drawing on his own experience of collecting folk traditions. A native of Glenorchy, McNicol was a poet in his own right, and he assisted Duncan Ban McIntyre in committing his work to writing. Oral versions of the hero tales were still being encountered in the Western Isles well into the nineteenth century by Alexander Carmichael, the Lismore-born tax official and compiler of *Carmina Gadelica* (Chapter 10).

The name of the most northerly, and grandest, cairn in the Lismore alignment provides another clue to Iron Age life on the island. When Gaelic became the dominant language, the Bronze Age was already more than a thousand years in the past but, with the naming of the cairn as Cnoc Aingeal (Fire Hillock, Plate 7a), the inhabitants were reflecting its long and continuous role in fire worship, shared by Bronze Age man and Iron Age Celt. Fire was the purifier, celebrated at Beltane on 1 May and Samhuinn on 1 November, by processions of people and livestock passing between the flames of bonfires to ensure a successful year. The household fire, kept lit all year, also assumed a spiritual importance, being quenched and renewed twice each year from these bonfires, a custom still preserved in parts of the Highlands well into the twentieth century (Chapter 8).

Bibliography

Armit, I. (2003) *Towers in the North*. Stroud: Tempus Publishing.

Heaney, M. (1994) *Over Nine Waves: A Book of Irish Legends*. London: Faber & Faber.

Hunter, F. (2006) 'New light on Iron Age massive armlets.' *Proceedings of the Society of Antiquaries of Scotland,* vol. 136, 135–60.

Jackson, K.H. (1964) *The Oldest Irish Tradition: A Window on the Iron Age*. Cambridge University Press (reprinted by Llanerch Publishers, 1999).

M'Lauchlan, T. (ed.) (1862) *Dean of Lismore's Book*. Edinburgh: Edmonston & Douglas.

4

Dalriada: Monks and Vikings

The 500 years from around AD 350 to 850 were momentous for Lismore, and also for Argyll as a whole: incorporation into the expanding Scots colony of Dalriada, including the change from P-Celtic to Gaelic language and culture; conversion to Christianity; contact with international traders; intermittent warfare amongst the competing kingdoms, culminating in the union of the Picts and Scots; and the onslaught of the Vikings, resulting in the withdrawal of political and religious authority and protection, and the collapse of security.

The Establishment of Dalriada

The northern tribes, occupying the mainland beyond the Forth–Clyde line, and the Northern and Western Islands, cannot be called Picts until around AD 300, when the Roman writer Eumenius first coined the term. This is not entirely an artificial date because the following period is associated with a flowering of Pictish art, in stone and metalwork, especially in the east and north of Pictland. Before that time, as the southern (Maeatae) and northern (Caledonii) tribes, they had waged sporadic war against the Roman invaders, who, although normally victorious, did not devote the resources to subdue and occupy such a large and intimidating kingdom when there were more pressing needs elsewhere in the empire. From around AD 160, the limit of permanent Roman authority lay at Hadrian's Wall, and peace was maintained partly by bribing the northern tribes, who regularly broke peace treaties, to raid the border region. There is evidence, such as the recycling of Roman metal by local bronze workers (as in the Lismore armlet), that this was also a period of trading between the northern tribes and the Romanised parts of the British Isles.

Fluctuation in Roman power in the fourth century had unexpected results. The Scots, still described as *from Ireland*, united with the Picts to raid the border area in at least four well-documented campaigns between 360 and 400. It is not entirely clear how the Scots, as an identifiable group, arose out of the indigenous Cruithne, but this period saw significant movement into Argyll from Ulster, as part of a pattern of active emigration from other parts of Ireland to Man and Wales, possibly in response to population pressures. Neither is it clear what motivated migration from relatively fertile Northern Ireland to the much less promising land of Argyll, but the dense clustering of duns, forts and brochs in Kintyre, Islay, Colonsay, mid-Argyll, Lorn and Lismore shows that they were not moving into an underpopulated area. It is possible that their leaders had a long-term strategy to use the colony as a bridgehead for challenging their allies, the Picts, who occupied extensive areas of good crop- and stock-rearing land in the eastern Lowlands; but it is more likely that they were invited over to be more readily mobilised in time of war. There is no evidence that this movement was other than peaceful.

The last major incursion of the Picts and Scots into the territory vacated by the Roman legions in the 450s marked the end of the alliance and, thereafter, there was intermittent conflict between them for 400 years, complicated by the northward advance of the Northumbrians (led by English-speaking Angles but probably involving a high proportion of the original Celtic population). The defeat of the P-Celtic-speaking Britons occupying the north of England and the Lothians (the kingdom of Gododdin) and the occupation of their strongholds on Traprain Law and Edinburgh Rock brought the Northumbrians into direct contact with South Pictland. These events, recorded in one of the earliest surviving poems in Welsh, *Y Gododdin*, dating from AD 600, resulted in a concentration of the Britons in Strathclyde, with their centre of power on Dumbarton Rock.

The traditional date for the founding of the Scots kingdom of Dalriada is 501, when the legendary Fergus mac Erc arrived from

Dalriada in Ireland to take control of what was already an extensive area stretching northwards from the initial colony in Kintyre to Mull and Appin. However, even as late as 563, Columba felt it necessary to seek the permission of the Pictish king, Bridei mac Maelcon, as well as the ruler of Dalriada to set up his monastery on Iona, but this may have been because the Scots had recently been heavily defeated in battle by Bridei. Further north, Lismore, an important centre of Iron Age and later Pictish religion, would not have been fully incorporated into the kingdom of the Scots before this date. The population on the island may well have remained predominantly Pictish, led by the occupants of Tirfuir and the many duns, but the culture of the Scots made rapid headway in Argyll, particularly in terms of language. Nevertheless, the two peoples were from the same genetic stock, and they were so similar in their way of life that archaeologists find it virtually impossible to discriminate between Pictish and Scottish occupation at sites in the west of Scotland (for example, at Dunadd and Dunollie).

Throughout its history, Dalriada in Alba (the Scots' name for 'Scotland' in Gaelic) remained a unified and centralised kingdom, allowing it to exert greater influence than might have been expected from its size. Its principal headquarters were on the great rock outcrop of Dunadd, developing from a modest Iron Age dun into a complex fortress that incorporated a ritual site associated with kingship. As its influence expanded northwards, three political units developed, controlled by powerful family groups. Lismore was part of the lands of the family of Loairn (Cenél Loairn), covering modern Lorn, Mull and probably parts of Morvern. By 575, following a convention at Drumceatt in Antrim said to have been facilitated by Columba, 'Scottish' Dalriada gained independence from its Irish parent. The Senchus Fer n-Alban (History of the Men of Scotland), an original document incorporated into later medieval Irish manuscripts, gives some clues to the success of the colony. It shows a high level of administration and an organised approach to the control of the seaways: part of the Senchus, a detailed military census, states that each unit of 20 'houses' was responsible for providing crews for two sea-going 'seven-bench' ships (14 rowers and a steersman), equipped to fight. The total muster for Cenél Loairn is estimated to be 600 fighting men, but the duties are listed under names rather than places and it is not possible to identify the resources expected of Lismore. At the very least, the island would have provided one ship and its crew.

Placed astride the western seaway and at the mouth of the Great Glen leading to eastern Pictland, Dalriada was in an ideal position to dominate the trade of the region. The results of excavation at Dunadd and the subordinate centre of power at Dunollie show that it was not slow to exploit the opportunities. The descriptions of visits by Gaulish traders in Adomnan's *Life of St Columba* are consistent with the recovery of fine pottery and glass from continental Europe from both sites, and scientific analysis of the pottery has revealed traces of herbs and dyestuffs from southern climates. Dunadd was also an important centre for the manufacture of fine jewellery and other items in bronze, silver and gold. Although much smaller than Pictland in terms of territory, productive agricultural land and population, Dalriada was compact, organised and increasingly wealthy.

Columba, Moluag and the Early Church

It will never be known why the Irish renounced paganism and embraced Christianity with apparent alacrity, after its introduction, according to tradition by Patrick, from Romanised Cumbria in the mid-fifth century. Explanations include the decline of druidism, the identification of Christ with the warrior gods of the Celtic world, and the fact that missionaries did not hesitate to adopt previously holy sites and convert pagan gods into Christian saints (most famously Saint Brigid, clearly a Mother Earth figure). What is clear is that, although the Celtic church developed ideals of peace and simplicity in its monasteries, it made little headway in moderating the activities of the warrior classes. Indeed, even if the legends implicating Columba in more than one bloody conflict in Ireland are unreliable, he was known to have prayed for the victory in battle of his chosen champions.

At least from the start of the reign of Fergus in 501, Dalriada would have been notionally a Christian kingdom, surrounded by pagan Picts, although the peaceful advance of the new faith into Pictland suggests that earlier British missionaries, allied to Ninian, may have prepared the way. A wave of Irish priests entered the

Pictland mission field in the sixth century, most of whom are entirely forgotten or appear in one or two church dedications or place names without any supporting documentation. Two celebrated missionaries, Columba and Lughaidh (most commonly in the form Moluag or 'my Lughaidh') arrived in Dalriada at exactly the same time (562 or 563), and each chose to set up a community of monks on a small island with strong traditions of pre-Christian religion. We know much more about Columba of Iona than Moluag of Lismore because he belonged to the Irish ruling class (specifically the Uí Néill); he made himself indispensable to the Kings of Dalriada by initiating their formal inauguration at Iona (Aidan in 574); and he had three devoted biographers or hagiographers, one of whom, at least, was a relation: Abbot Cummene (died 669), Abbot Adomnan (704) and the Venerable Bede (735) from the daughter abbey of Lindisfarne. Most of what we know about Moluag was originally transmitted orally, although his historical reality is firmly anchored by a few entries in Irish annals and a range of early dedications and place names.

Moluag, from the seminary at Bangor in Northern Ireland, outside Dalriada (in Antrim), is reputed to have landed at Port Moluag, on the east coast of Lismore, near the modern farm of Baileouchdarach and close to Tirfuir. This was a logical point of arrival because his party would have had to secure the approval of the local chief, presumably resident at the broch. The traditional story attached to his arrival is less convincing, as different versions have been used in the celebration of a range of Celtic heroes. It is said that Moluag and Columba were competing to acquire the territory of Lismore as a base for their missionary activities and that they were actually racing in coracles to get there first. Seeing that Columba was likely to win, Moluag cut off his little finger and threw it ashore so that his 'blood and flesh' could claim the island first. Columba is reported to have been spiteful in defeat: 'may the rocks grow with edges uppermost and may you have only alder for fuel'. Moluag, fully aware of the rockiness of the island and the poor quality of alder wood, was content to rely on miracles: 'the rocks will not hurt to walk upon and alder will burn like tinder'.

Thereafter it was Moluag's island, although legends also record that Columba was active on the tidal island of Bernera. A later story tells that Campbell of Lochnell was repeatedly punished by tragic accidents for building a staircase in his castle out of an ancient yew under which Columba had preached. Although yews are rare on Lismore there are still at least two on Bernera, but not quite of the size for joinery work. It seems strange that there should have been such intense competition among those engaged in a common cause, but there is other evidence of priestly conflict in Dalriada, such as the early establishment of three different churches on Tiree, named for Columba, Moluag and Comgall.

Moluag established his *muinntir* (centre for education and support of the mission) near the present parish church, and at the centre of an area that had been devoted to ritual by the Picts and earlier societies. Nearby hillocks, named in Gaelic (Cnoc na Breithe – the Trial Hill, north-west of the church; Druim a'Chrochaidh – Gallows Ridge, south), indicate that this was also an ancient place for the exercise of law. It has been suggested that, as on Iona, the pattern of fields in the area follows the line of the original ditch demarcating the abbey lands, and the Sanctuary or Swan Stone (Clach na h-Ealamh; Figure 6.1) to the east of the present church may mark part of the central perimeter where asylum seekers could find protection. Tradition has it that those who managed to touch the stone would be immune from prosecution for a year and a day. The Black Cross of Lismore, set up in the churchyard by Moluag's successor as abbot (St Dudhoc or McGhilleDhuibh, said to be the origin of the Lismore family name of Black), was probably destroyed at the Reformation and only its plinth remains. Close to the baptismal stone (Chapter 2), it was a focal point for local celebrations such as the proclaiming of marriage banns.

On Lismore, Moluag was in a good position, near the mouth of the Great Glen, to evangelise northern Pictland, setting up daughter *muinntirs* at Rosemarkie in Easter Ross and Mortlach in Moray, which continued as principal church centres in later centuries. There are churches dedicated to Moluag in Lewis, Skye, Raasay, Tiree, Mull, Morvern, Invernesshire, Aberdeenshire and elsewhere. At least some of these reflect the activities of Moluag himself and his monks, and it has even been claimed that he completed a voyage to Iceland. He died, in old age, in 592 at the hermitage of Ardclach in Moray, where the monks kept a boat to ferry travellers across the treacherous River Findhorn, and it is likely that his remains were returned for burial on Lismore.

Moluag's personal reputation has never been challenged; in the Martyrology of Oengus, a day-by-day celebration of saints, Moluag appears for 25 June (the date his death), with the description:

> The pure, the bright, the pleasant
> The sun of Lismore
> That is Moluag of Lismore in Alba.

The interpretation of his name in Gaelic is 'gleaming light'. Here again, the sun features, as in Bronze Age religion.

Although his life history is sketchy, there are at least four extant reminders of Moluag in modern Lismore. Moluag's chair, a natural stone structure, whose arms were damaged by a modern roadman, is where he is said to have rested by the roadside near Baligarve. Moluag's well is enclosed by a wooden fence to the east of the church. More surprisingly, after nearly 1,500 years, part of Moluag's crozier does survive – a curved piece of blackthorn wood, around 85cm long and studded with bronze nails which fixed the original gilded copper covering, now lost. This covering is the explanation of one of its names, the yellow stick. The crozier, the bachuil of St Moluag (Plate 9), is in the care of the Livingstone Barons of Bachuil, who hold a charter for this responsibility dating from the sixteenth century (Chapter 7), but maintain that there is a continuous line back to the first guardian or dewar, who served Moluag himself. The bachuil, which has been used over the centuries in the blessing of man, beast and boat, is on view, by appointment, at Bachuil House, near the church.

There are good historical reasons to believe that the ancient iron bell found at Kilmichael Glassary (Plate 8b), protected by a later medieval bell shrine, dates from the time of Moluag. The associated legend requires more faith: the smith who was asked to manufacture the bell refused because he lacked the necessary charcoal but Moluag insisted on using rushes for fuel instead, and the work was done to his satisfaction. It is also likely that Moluag (or one of his contemporaries at this time of arrival of Gaelic) was the originator of the name by which the island was known from his time onwards, Lios Mòr: Gaelic for 'the great garden' (recognising its fertility), 'the great enclosure' (Moluag's abbey enclosure), or even 'the great fortress' (referring to the ring of fortified roundhouses).

We know little about the subsequent life of the abbey on Lismore, compared to the well-documented Iona, apart from a list of early abbots, but the evidence on the ground shows that much of the island was devoted to religious activity (Figure 4.1). Of three

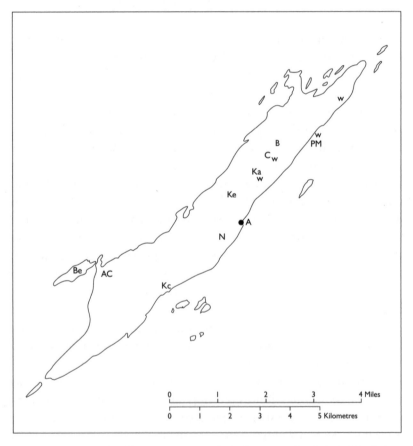

FIGURE 4.1 Early Christian sites: A Achnacroish; AC Achinduin Castle; B Bachuil House; Be Bernera; C the site of the cathedral and St Moluag's *muinntir*; Ka Killandrist; Ke Killean; Kc Kilcheran; N Newfield (Cill an-t Suidhe); PM Port Moluag; the ancient wells (w) are (from north to south) Tobar Mhuire, Tobar na Slainte, St Moluag's and St Andrew's.

surviving dedications, one to a major Irish saint, a colleague of
Columba, and the others to two apostles – Kilcheran (Cill Chiaran,
the cell of Ciaran), Killean (Cill Iain, John) and Killandrist (Cill
Anndraist, Andrew) – two are associated with traces of church or
burial ground enclosures, although the earthwork attributed to
Killean (Cill an-t Suidhe at Newfield, damaged by ploughing up
in the early nineteenth century) could actually be much older. A
spring near Killandist has traditionally been known as St Andrew's
Well, and the place name Achnacroish (Achadh na Croise – Field of
the Cross, presumably referring to another ancient burial ground)
underlines the importance of the central part of the island in
Christian observance. There have also been suggestions, difficult
to substantiate, of early church buildings on Bernera and Ramsay
Island.

It is possible that the three 'cells' relate to a community
of Culdees, who, from around AD 700 for up to 300 years,
continued the traditions of independent and ascetic monasticism
in isolated places, after both Dalriada and Pictland had adopted
the organisation and structure of the Roman church. What is
clear is that the Christian presence was strong and enduring,
and that much of the economy of the island must have been
devoted to supporting the life of the church. Again, unlike Iona,
there appears to have been no tradition of wealthy endowment
of Moluag's Abbey, although the name Appin does suggest that
the area might have been the 'abbot's land'; and there is no
record of fine craftsmanship, such as manuscript illumination,
apart from the fragments of a fine eighth-century grave slab now
preserved in the island museum (Plate 10). The impression is of a
workaday community whose modest possessions would not have
been particularly attractive to raiding Vikings. But its reputation
for holiness convinced the church authorities in the thirteenth
century that it was the appropriate place for the new bishopric of
Argyll.

Union of the Picts and Scots

In the traditional schoolbook account of the uniting of Picts
and Scots under Kenneth mac Alpin, forming a nucleus for the

emergence of the country of Scotland, the Scots defeated the Picts and imposed their king and language. Modern research has shown that this picture is simplistic and misleading, ignoring the chaotic struggle amongst the various peoples in the area, including the Northumbrians, the extent of kinship amongst the various rulers, and the importance of pure chance in the timing of events, particularly the arrival of the Vikings.

During the seventh century it looked as if the English-speaking Northumbrians would become the dominant group in the region. In 603 Aethelfrith defeated Aidan, King of the Scots, and invaded South Pictland; by 668 Northumbria had annexed parts of Dalriada and occupied Fife but, at the battle at Dunnichen (Nechtansmere) in Angus in 685, Bridei mac Bili, King of the Picts, drove the Northumbrians back beyond the Forth. The eighth century was very turbulent. King-lists show that Oengus, King of the Picts from 729, took control of Dalriada from 741 but failed to extend his authority to cover the kingdom of Strathclyde (which remained independent until the fortress on Dumbarton Rock was sacked by Vikings around 870). The joint kingdom lasted until 778 and, again, from 800 to 839, Constantine and his son ruled over both Dalriada and Pictland. Meanwhile, the Vikings had occupied Orkney and Shetland, both originally under the control of Pictland, and, from this base, had begun their raids on the west coast down to Ireland, attacking Iona in 795 and on at least three more occasions in the following 30 years. The advance of the Vikings into Caithness and Sutherland and their devastation of South Pictland from a third direction, the south-east, in 839, resulting in the death of the King of Dalriada and the sons of the King of Pictland, may well have been the decisive political factor in the union of Dalriada and Pictland in 843 or 844 under Kenneth mac Alpin.

This series of events indicates that, as would be expected from its size and resources, Pictland dominated the region, finally curbing the advance of the Angles and providing the leadership for Dalriada during much of the period. It was, however, increasingly weakened by Viking aggression around its extensive coastline. Among Celtic peoples there was a strong tradition of binding ruling families together by exchanging children in fostering arrangements and of sealing treaties by marriage. For example, the father of the Pictish king in the time of Columba and Moluag, Bridei mac Maelcon, has been identified as a Welsh-speaking Briton. The result of these interrelationships was that, by the time Kenneth mac Alpin united the weakened Picts and the Scots into a single kingdom, he was a member of a ruling class that could not be defined as Pictish or Scottish, but it was predominantly Gaelic-speaking and had adopted the Scots' tradition of inheritance through the male line. The triumph of the Scots was, therefore, more cultural than military. The important, and unfortunate, result for Lismore and the rest of the western seaboard was that, in the face of the Viking onslaught in the west, they lost the effective organisation of Dalriada. The king withdrew to the greater safety of South Pictland, to Forteviot near Perth, and the leaders of Cenél Loairn moved to establish a powerful dynasty in Moray, leaving a power vacuum that lasted for 300 years until it was finally filled by Somerled and his successors.

Viking Lismore

Long before the Viking Age, which started in the late eighth century, the fertility of the people of Scandinavia exceeded the capacity of its soils to feed them, and waves of Langobards, Rugii, Goths and other tribes flooded south, joining the many 'barbarians' pressing on the Roman Empire. These migrations were mainly overland but, by around 750, the restless people of the north had developed new technology that opened the possibility of long voyages. The Viking ship, with its strong but flexible construction, shallow draught, and improvements in rigging and sails, was fast, safe and robust, equally suited to the open sea and inland waterways. The Gokstad ship, built in the eighth century, and recovered almost intact from a ship burial in Vestfold in Norway, is a classic example of the type: 23m long and 5.25m at its broadest, it had seating for 16 pairs of rowers, and room for two teams, with a total crew of up to 70. Regular voyages into the Atlantic, and eventually as far as Iceland, Greenland and North America, now became practical.

Lismore, on the direct seaway from Orkney to Man and Ireland, could not have avoided the attentions of the Vikings. Once past

Ardnamurchan, ships entered more sheltered waters in the lee of Mull, Jura and Islay, and there were protected anchorages, for example at Kerrera. The early Vikings, predominantly Norwegians, were on the hunt for portable valuables and slaves but they would also take advantage of food supplies on their way, and their onslaught was particularly frightening because of its novelty. Warfare between the Picts and Scots is known to have been fully amphibious, in small galleys such as the 'seven-bench' ships in the Dalriada census, but each Viking ship was bigger and faster, and able to land a sizeable fighting band directly on to sandy or pebbly beaches. There was little time to organise defence, and the element of surprise was greater because these were independent units of one or more ships, striking at will rather than participating in more organised warfare. What was most chilling, as far as the early chroniclers were concerned, was that they showed no respect for the church; in fact, because of their endowments (fine metalwork, jewelled bindings, illuminated manuscripts), the undefended monasteries were a favourite target. Eventually, the surviving relics and manuscripts at Iona were withdrawn to Kells in Ireland and Dunkeld in Perthshire.

However, it was not long before some of the raiders began to settle in the Western Islands, particularly in Lewis and Skye, but also further south. Viking graves from the ninth and tenth centuries have been discovered on many of the Argyll islands (Coll, Tiree, Mull, Colonsay, Oronsay, Islay and Gigha). They are readily identified because they contain 'grave goods', a practice uncommon in the area after the Bronze Age, and these items are usually recognisably Scandinavian. As most of the burials, including Norse females with their characteristic jewellery, are in readily cultivated *machair* land, it has been concluded that these people were resident farmers, some arriving in family units within decades of the first raids around AD 800. No Viking graves have been found on Lismore, but the discovery of a Norse pin and boat rivets during excavations at Tirfuir suggests that they took possession of the broch. Further south, a fragment of Viking gold jewellery was found at Kilcheran.

The principal Lismore legend of Viking times centres round Coeffin (otherwise Chaifen or Chabin), where a Norse fortress on the site of the later medieval castle was occupied by a Norwegian leader of the same name. His sister, Beothal, dying of sorrow at the death in battle of her betrothed, haunts him until he agrees to bring her body all the way back to Norway for burial with her dead lover. However, in the process of washing and preparing her bones, he manages to leave a little finger bone (or a little toe bone) behind, and it continues the haunting until a second arduous voyage is completed. The unusual name of the township of Baleveolan may commemorate her name, and it is interesting that the little finger features here as with Moluag. This legend may be part of a common thread in the West Highlands and Islands, developing unique features in different areas; for example, there is a dun on Gigha named after Chibhich or Keefi, who is interpreted as either a Viking or Pictish hero. Another oral tradition is that, when there was early warning of Viking raids on Lismore, all the cattle of the island were rounded up and driven to Park in the north of the island. Big Eilidh is celebrated as the woman who, instead, hid her cow near home at Baligrundle and drove off the raiders single-handedly with her flail.

Without first-hand records of the impact of either the raiding Vikings or the succeeding Norse settlers, the best evidence is from place names, and their relative scarcity on Lismore suggests that the impact was less than overwhelming. Vikings arriving for the first time by sea would have named prominent coastal landmarks as reference points for navigation, but these would not have passed into general use, for transmission down the ages, unless the newcomers went on to settle the land. Taking the suffix -ay or -a as a key to Scandinavian names for islands, of the many round Lismore only a few are recognisable among the preponderance of Gaelic names: Ramsay, Bernera, Pladda and the isolated rock Branra opposite Port Moluag. Interpretation of these names is speculative (Ram's or Raven's island; Björn's island), but Pladda is clearly 'Flat Island'. The hybrid name of a fifth island, Eilean Musdile, is intriguing, suggesting 'Mouse Valley'. Surprisingly, Norse names for the most conspicuous features of the coast, including Eilean Dubh (Dark Island), the spectacular Eilean na Cloiche (Island of the Stone), and Sailean (The Inlet), have not survived.

The impression that Lismore was not densely settled by Norse speakers is confirmed by the low frequency of farm and settlement names. There are two foci in the southern half of the island: Baligrundle (combining the Gaelic for 'township' with the Norse

'Green Valley'); and Frackersaig (interpreted as 'Spearsman's Bay' but it could equally be the more prosaic 'Trader's Bay'), with Birgidile ('Brigid's Valley') further inland. Fiart (possibly 'Further'), near the south end, may also be of Norse origin but, elsewhere, the names of farms and physical features are overwhelmingly Gaelic. From place-name evidence, therefore, it looks as if a handful of Norse settlers took possession of some of the best farmland, as well as the best anchorage at Port Ramsay. Although a minority, they may have dominated the life of the island by force. Things might have been very different, with successive waves of Scandinavians occupying the western seaboard, if the Hebridean Norse had not turned their attentions to settling the virgin lands of Iceland towards the end of the ninth century.

In the last few years, historians of the Viking period have been given an unexpected and powerful new tool in the form of geographical distributions of DNA types. There are clear differences between Scandinavians and Atlantic Celts in the DNA patterns of their Y-chromosomes (carried only by males) and of their mitochondria (transmitted only by females). Comparing the frequency of theses two types in indigenous people (recognised by establishing the place of birth of the grandparents) it has been possible to estimate the proportions of Norse men and women settling in different parts of Scotland and Iceland. Nearly half of the men and women in modern Shetland, and around one-third of those in Orkney, are of Norse descent, demonstrating a major settlement of families, with nearly equal numbers of men and women. The proportion of men in the Western Isles and Skye with Viking ancestors is lower, around 20 per cent, but that of women is even lower (around 10 per cent), indicating a greater degree of intermarriage between single Vikings and Celtic women. The most striking result of the analysis is that, although 75 per cent of Icelandic males are of Viking descent, only around one-third of the women are. This is a satisfying confirmation of the tradition that the Norse settlers in Iceland were predominantly from Scotland and Ireland, reducing their genetic impact on the islands, and that they took their women from the local population as wives or slaves.

Because the analysis of the rest of the western seaboard of Scotland is over a much greater area, it is not possible to draw any firm conclusions about the Argyll islands, apart from the fact that both male and female Viking ancestors contribute less than 15 per cent of the gene pool. The merging of this minority of Norse leaders with the Celtic majority created a hybrid population, the Gall-Gaedhil or 'Foreign Gaels', with loyalties divided among Norway, Scotland, Irish chiefs and local leaders; they dominated the politics of the area, culminating in the rise of Somerled.

Bibliography

Bannerman, J. (1974) *Studies in the History of Dalriada.* Edinburgh: Scottish Academic Press.

Goodacre, S., Helgason, A., Nicholson, J., Southam, L., Ferguson, L., Hickey, E., Vega, E., Stefánsson, K., Ward, R. and Sykes, B., (2005) 'Genetic evidence for a family-based Scandinavian settlement of Shetland and Orkney during the Viking periods.' *Heredity* 95: 129–35.

Laing, L. and Laing, J. (1993) *The Picts and the Scots.* Stroud: Alan Sutton Publishing.

Roesdahl, E. (1998) *The Vikings.* 2nd edn. London: Penguin

Sharpe, R. (trans.) (1991) *Adomnan of Iona. Life of St Columba.* London: Penguin Classics.

Woolf, A. (2007) *From Pictland to Alba, 789–1070.* Edinburgh: Edinburgh University Press.

5

ᴑᵘ̲

Somerled and the MacDougalls

T he eastward migration of the leading families of Dalriada in the face of the Viking onslaught opened up a political fault-line between the mainland and the western seaboard, whose influence can be felt even today. For the next 400 years, up to the Treaty of Perth in 1266, when the Norwegian king surrendered the Hebrides to the Scottish crown, the two areas pursued different objectives. Successive kings of Alba (Dalriada and Pictland) sought to bring all of the people of the mainland under their rule and to extend their influence further south into English territory. Once they had reduced the threat to their shores from Viking raids, their interest in the western fringes was aroused only during periodic incursions by the Gall-Gaedhil into their territory. Until they had subdued the troublesome areas of Moray and Galloway, and wrested Caithness and Sutherland from the Norse Earls of Orkney, acquisition of the western seaboard was low on their agenda.

Meanwhile, the Hebrides (the Sudreyjar or Sudreys, the Southern Isles including Arran, Bute and Man, as distinct from the Northern Isles of Shetland and Orkney), were part of an essentially Scandinavian world, stretching from Norway to Ireland, where the market in Dublin did a lively trade in Celtic slaves. For much of this period, their rulers had a primary loyalty to Norway and they intermarried with their Norse and Irish neighbours; but the practical difficulties involved in rule from Bergen meant that they enjoyed considerable independence. Having been used to independence, they found it difficult to accept the authority of the Scottish crown, and this eventually resulted in a long struggle between successive Lords of the Isles and the Stewart kings (Chapters 6, 7), who

43

were hampered by the same logistic problems as their Norwegian predecessors. These practical issues were compounded by the differences in culture and society that arose out of the increasingly European orientation of Scotland (including approaches to law and ownership of property) and the Scandinavian orientation of the west. However, this was not a linguistic divide, as Gaelic came to dominate over Norse in the west and over Pictish in the east.

Lismore lay at the meeting of these two worlds. As well as peaceful travel and trading, the relentless raiding and outright war in the region were conducted principally by sea, and the small Hebridean galley (the 12- to 20-oared birlinn) would have been a common sight round its shores. Possibly only once in a generation, a great fleet of war galleys, including longships, would cruise past the south end, seeking shelter in the lee of Kerrera. Since Magnus Bareleg, King of Norway, could have circumnavigated the island in 1098, Lismore may well have been part of the Sudreyjar at that time. The fertility of the island must have made it a favoured target of raiders, although in the twelfth century it probably came under the active protection of mainland Lorn, which was not heavily settled by the Norse, and it certainly belonged to the empire of Somerled. As we shall see in later chapters, Lismore passed from the MacDougalls to the Stewarts and finally to the Campbells; its fate in the many conflicts from the Scottish War of Independence up to the Jacobite rebellion of 1745 tended to be different from those of the surrounding areas.

Because of the ultimate success of the Canmore dynasty in bringing together the different components of modern Scotland and the marginalisation of the seaboard in later centuries, the history of the west has been both neglected and distorted. Had the Norwegians and Danes concentrated their efforts on mainland Scotland rather than Iceland, eastern England and Normandy, it could well have evolved into a Scandinavian country. It is also true that the modern distribution of population, wealth and trade in Scotland tends to obscure the importance of the area in medieval times. In pre-industrial Scotland, up to half of the population lived in the Highlands and Islands. Much of the medieval history of the area has been, until recently, based on oral sources such as clan histories but there has been an encouraging increase in interest in the demanding work of piecing together the story from monkish annals, sagas and other written sources from Scandinavia, Ireland, England and elsewhere in Europe. A great deal of information is revealed by studies of modern DNA.

Lismore, and most other parts of Argyll, do not figure strongly in the few surviving documents or the archaeology of the period. Indeed, there is a long break of more than a thousand years between the building of the broch at Tirfuir and the start of work on the medieval castles and cathedral in the thirteenth century. It is tempting to conclude that the roundhouses continued to be used during much of this period, and there is archaeological evidence to support the idea, particularly from Tirfuir Broch. The aim of this chapter is to provide an overview of the late- and post-Viking years on the western seaboard so that the thread of the story of Lismore can be picked up in the twelfth century when historical records become available.

Somerled

The bands of Vikings that sailed the western coasts were independent and free to raid and settle where they could, but, by the time of the evacuation of Dalriada by its rulers, the names of local leaders of the Gall-Gaedhil and the term Innsegall (the Islands of the Foreigners, otherwise the Hebrides) were beginning to make their appearance in Irish annals. Some idea of the appalling insecurity of the times, and the level of violence, can be gained from reports of the shipping of 200 boatloads of slaves to Dublin after the siege of the British fort of Dumbarton in 871. The King of Norway tried to deal with the turbulence in the area by sending his son to Dublin in 853. Olaf had some success, including the defeat of Ketil Flatnose, Chief of Innsegall, in 857 but the direct authority of Norway fluctuated over the following decades until around 950, when the Earls (or Jarls) of Orkney took control.

In a period of complex and poorly understood history, several events took place in the eleventh century that had great significance for the political future of Argyll and the Western Isles. The bloody Battle of Clontarf near Dublin in 1014 was a decisive victory for the forces of the High King of Ireland, Brian Boru, over the King of Leinster, supported by Sigurd, Earl of Orkney, and groups of Norse mercenaries from all along the seaboard of Scotland including, apparently, men from Argyll. This weakened the control of Orkney over the Sudreyjar, but the death of Brian led to further civil war in Ireland, leaving the field clear for the eventual emergence, in 1079, of a powerful and durable kingdom of Man and the Isles, incorporating all of the islands up to Lewis in the north, under Godred Crovan, son of Harold the Black of Islay. Meanwhile, on the mainland, King Malcolm II, whose territory already included the British kingdom of Strathclyde, had finally defeated the Northumbrians at Carham in 1034, fixing the border of Scotland at the Tweed. There remained unresolved problems in Galloway and the far north, but successive Kings of Scots could now start to pay attention to their western borders.

Clearly, Norse control of the north and west of the British Isles was faltering, prompting the first royal visit from Norway in more than 200 years. By 1098 Magnus Bareleg was confident enough of his position at home to sail for Orkney, dispossessing the incumbent jarl and sending him back to Norway. He then embarked with 160 ships to cruise the islands from Lewis to Islay, causing devastation all the way, except on Iona, which was spared. Dislodging the Crovan king in Man, he then proceeded to raid North Wales. At some point, a treaty was concluded with envoys of the new King of Scots (Edgar), who formally surrendered all of the islands to the west that Magnus could circumnavigate with a rudder in place. This led to the legendary crossing by boat of the narrow neck of land at Tarbert, Loch Fyne, suggesting that Kintyre should also belong to Norway.

In the course of harrying the west, Magnus seems to have driven out Gillebride mac Gilledomnan, who had established his authority over part of the debatable land between Scotland and the Innsegall, probably including Ardnamurchan, Morvern and parts of Lorn, Lismore and Mull. This Gall-Gaedhil leader, originally from a family based in Islay, found sanctuary in Ireland, where his son Somerled was born around 1100. Although King Magnus was back in 1103, his death in Ulster meant that the authority of the Norwegian crown was again undermined, with the descendants of Godred Crovan resuming control over Man and Innsegall and dispossessed leaders such as Gillebride moving back into their former lands. As it turned out, Gillebride proved to be ineffectual, and oral traditions picture his family seeking refuge in a cave in Morvern. Reaching manhood, Somerled became the chosen leader and he is reputed to have defeated the resident Scandinavians in Morvern and Ardnamurchan at least partly by clever subterfuge: instructing his men to move into and out of sight in different clothing, he tricked his enemies into overestimating the forces under his command.

Whatever the truth of these traditions, Somerled must have been a master of the diplomatic as well as the military arts because, by the 1130s, he was effectively the ruler of most of the original mainland area of Dalriada, Lismore and Mull, yet on good terms with his powerful immediate neighbours. In spite of gaining control of a sizeable area of mainland Scotland, he appears to have been viewed by David I as a valuable force for order in the west, and his recognition of the authority of the King of Scots is confirmed by the presence of men from Lorn and the Isles, possibly even himself, in the army that fought against the English at the Battle of the Standard in 1138. Somerled's firm adherence to Christianity, including his support for Iona, where his daughter Bethoc was the founding abbess of the Augustinian nunnery, must have recommended him to David, the sponsor of so many abbeys. Nevertheless, he held out against the prevailing policy of Normanisation. By marrying Ragnhild, daughter of Olaf, King of Man, around 1140, he protected himself against possible attack from the west and north and underlined his affiliation with the Gall-Gaedhil. Their descendants were to dominate in the west for the next 300 years.

The political situation suddenly became more challenging in 1153. The almost simultaneous deaths of David I and Olaf of Man, murdered by his nephews, removed two trusted allies, but they also forced Somerled to take up arms to deal with family obligations. Godred arrived back in Man to avenge the murder of his father, but he proved to be a tyrant. In deciding to act against Godred, Somerled must have been motivated by family interest (Godred was his brother-in-law), but also by the opportunity to expand his empire. Proclaiming his eldest son, Dugall, to be Lord of the Isles, he threw down a challenge that Godred could not ignore.

However, at the same time, his relations with the Scottish crown were compromised by a rebellion against the new 12-year-old king, Malcolm IV, by Somerled's nephews, the sons of Malcolm MacHeth and his sister; they had, presumably, been fostered by Somerled in the absence of Malcolm, imprisoned for much of his life for an earlier rebellion in Moray. The details of the abortive rebellion have not survived but the chronicles of the period show that, from that time, Somerled was considered to be a potential rebel and, because of his policy of not forming alliances with the increasingly Normanised Scottish ruling class, he had no allies at court. In spite of his support of the Church, the Augustinian and Cistercian monks who drew up the chronicles of the time had no sympathy with those they saw as barbarians in the west.

After the MacHeth rebellion had been crushed, the Argyll seaborne forces were mobilised, presumably including ships from Lismore, for a showdown with Godred, the King of Man. The two fleets met on the night of 5 January 1156 off the coast of Islay in an appalling and inconclusive slaughter later known as the Battle of the Lord's Epiphany. In subsequent negotiations, Godred surrendered all the islands south of Ardnamurchan to Somerled. Later, in 1158, Somerled completed the work by invading Man, and taking control of all of its territories, except perhaps Lewis and Harris. Approaching 60 years of age, he was at the height of his powers.

Somerled took part in a Christmas feast at Perth in 1160, apparently making peace with the King of Scots (the feudal lord at least for his mainland territory), but developments in the west were to drive him into a course of action that led to his death. In the process of 'Europeanising' Scotland, David I had introduced Norman, Breton and Flemish knights as bulwarks against the Celtic or Gall-Gaedhil areas in Argyll, Galloway and Moray. In particular, the Stewarts were granted extensive lands around Renfrew, driving a wedge between Argyll and Galloway, from which they were encouraged to expand northwards, establishing strongholds in Bute and Cowal. Somerled's rising in 1164, supported by mercenaries from as far away as Dublin, appears to have been a misguided attempt to limit the ambitions of the Stewarts. Advancing up the Clyde, Somerled's force was surprised at Renfrew and both he and his natural son Gillecom were killed.

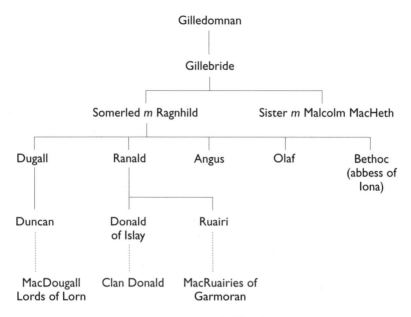

FIGURE 5.1 Somerled family tree.

The MacSorleys

The consequences for his sons of Somerled's attack on the Stewarts might have been much more serious had Malcolm IV not died soon after. His successor, William the Lion, ruling from 1165 to 1214, had ambitions to reclaim land in the north of England. These led to disaster, but he was later effective in subduing Galloway and securing the mainland areas formerly occupied by the Earl of Orkney. Somerled's successors were generally left to their own quarrelsome devices.

At his death, Somerled was effective ruler over the mainland from Kintyre to Knoydart, and the islands from Islay to the Uists, having lost control of Man. Arran, Bute and much of Cowal were now firmly in the hands of the Scottish crown and Norman knights. The distribution of Somerled's territory amongst his three surviving sons, the MacSorleys, was complicated, and changed over the following century. In what appears to be the original division, Dugall, the eldest and the progenitor of the MacDougall Lords of Lorn, received the heartland: Lorn, Benderloch, Lismore, Mull, Coll and Tiree. Ranald, the founder of all the branches of Clan Donald, was given Kintyre, Ardnamurchan, Morvern, Islay and Jura. Angus received Garmoran (Moidart, Arisaig, Morar, Knoydart, Rum, Eigg, the Uists, Barra and Benbecula), and he may have inherited claims to Bute, Arran and Skye. During their lifetimes there was considerable conflict and some redistribution. In 1210 Angus and his male heirs were all killed; Garmoran passed to Ranald, and, on his death, his son Donald inherited Islay, Kintyre and the Isles, while Ruairi took Garmoran. Although the MacRuairis were influential in the thirteenth century, the male line died out and the sole heiress married back into the main MacDonald line, founding the Clanranald branch.

The legal basis on which the MacSorleys held these lands was complicated and uncertain. In principle, for lands on the mainland, they were feudal subjects of the Kings of Scots and, for the islands, they were answerable to the Kings of Norway, who were absorbed in civil war at home for much of the twelfth century. In practice, logistical problems meant that they were effectively independent. This relatively informal arrangement lasted until the accession of Alexander II, the first Scottish king with the ambition and opportunity to take control of the west.

The hundred years from the death of Somerled in 1164 were characterised in the isles by continual unrest, with the MacRuairis possibly being the worst offenders, and by the steady incursion of the apparatus and agents of the Scottish crown into the west. By 1220 the kings of both countries were becoming more actively engaged in solving the perceived problems of the area, and this eventually led to conflict. In 1221 the young King Alexander II led an armed force into Argyll but was frustrated by extreme weather. Nevertheless, this sign that he was serious in his wish to control the western seaboard, and the arrival of emissaries from the isles complaining about the behaviour of the MacDougalls, motivated Håkon Håkonsson, King of Norway, to send a fleet under Uspak (an enigmatic individual, probably a Gall-Gaedhil) to enforce Norwegian rule. However, the early death of Uspak nullified any effects of his campaign, whose main achievement had been the occupation of Bute. Alexander II opened negotiations with Håkon in 1244 to buy the Sudreyjar, without success. The stage was set for a second military invasion of the west by the King of Scots.

Norway and Scotland, 1249–66

To place the events of 1249 in context, it is important to understand that, although the MacSorleys were ambitious, ruthless and violent, they were also strong supporters of the Church, and very active in introducing the new monastic orders in their area. In one of the very few documents referring to Dugall, son of Somerled, he is recorded as a witness in Durham in 1175. There are several interpretations of his presence, but it could well have been in connection with the establishment of the community of Benedictines at Iona. In the years after the death of their father, the MacSorleys were also involved in achieving Somerled's ambition of setting up a new Cistercian monastery at Saddell in Kintyre. Later, around 1220, Dugall's son Duncan founded Ardchattan for the Valliscaulians. At this time, the islands belonged to the diocese of Sodor and Man, normally subject to the bishop in Trondheim (Nidaros) in Norway, whereas mainland Argyll was under Dunkeld. Towards the end of the twelfth century, probably under pressure from Somerled's sons, Dugall and Ranald, the diocese of Argyll, from the Clyde to Loch Broom, was separated from Dunkeld. Certainly by 1225 the seat of its bishop was on Lismore.

All was not well at the start of the new bishopric. Building the cathedral did not start until around 1250, endowments were scarce or diverted from their intended use, and the post of Bishop of Argyll was vacant for long periods. After a long vacancy, William, chancellor to the Bishop of Moray, was elected and consecrated in 1240, but he was drowned within a year of his appointment. Alexander II was very concerned about this situation, and planned to transfer the bishop's seat to the mainland. In 1249 he mustered a substantial naval force and travelled with his court and advisers into Argyll with the joint aims of bringing the MacDougalls into line and resolving the Lismore crisis.

This was not a good moment for Ewen MacDougall, Lord of Argyll, great-grandson of Somerled. He had been summoned by Håkon to Bergen on the occasion of the marriage of the King of Man, to pay homage on behalf of the Isles and this had, apparently, been approved by King Alexander. However, with the loss of the marriage party on their voyage home, Ewen was dispatched to Man to hold the fort until the succession could be arranged. In giving priority to the needs of Håkon, he neglected his duty to Alexander, who, before his unexpected and untimely death on Kerrera, demanded that he surrender his lands and castles. These included the new stone castle at Dunstaffnage, the outstanding fortress of the area, probably started by Duncan but completed by Ewen.

Following the debacle at Kerrera, Ewen was in disgrace for several years, in a time of progressive penetration of the west by the Scottish crown. The king acquired lands and a royal castle on Loch Awe, on the marches of MacDougall territory, and the crown was strongly represented to the north-west by the powerful Norman Comyn Earls of Badenoch and Lochaber. Ewen responded by cooperating with Alexander III, the first of the MacSorleys to do so, and he was rewarded by the restoration of his lands by 1260. Later, the marriage of his heir, Alexander (named after the king), to the daughter of the Earl of Badenoch was probably the first such alliance with the Norman aristocracy among the MacSorleys, and was to have grave consequences for the MacDougalls.

During the 1250s, Håkon, tiring of the persistent diplomatic missions from Scotland to buy the Hebrides, decided to take matters into his own hands. Leaving late in the year in 1263, he brought a great armada of ships to the Northern Isles, cruising through the Western Isles from Skye to Kerrera and on to Gigha during August. To ensure success in establishing his right to the Sudreyjar, he needed the practical support of the three main leaders: Dugald MacRuairi (Garmoran), Ewen MacDougall and Angus of Islay. Dugald was an enthusiastic supporter, used by Håkon to threaten Kintyre in order to bring Angus into the venture, but Ewen refused to take part in action against his feudal superior. Håkon detained Ewen for some time, to act as an emissary to the Scottish king, but later released him unharmed when they reached the Clyde. The fact that Ewen avoided being summarily executed by Håkon testifies to his outstanding diplomatic skills, and his usefulness to both kings.

The rest of the story is familiar: Håkon, with a great naval force, was unable to come to grips with the Scottish king's army on land, although Dugald led a fleet of between 40 and 60 ships up Loch Long and across to Loch Lomond at Tarbert and then raided Lennox, the possession of the hated Stewarts. With the weather deteriorating in late September, several of the invading ships were wrecked near Largs, and the Scottish army won a minor skirmish on the beach. Sailing north, Håkon rewarded Dugald with Ewen's lands, but he was not to enjoy them for long. The great Norwegian hero king Håkon Håkonsson died on his way home on Orkney, and his successor lost interest in the Hebrides, sending a series of envoys to Scotland, culminating in the Treaty of Perth in July 1266. With Norway giving up all claims to the Sudreyjar, Lismore, restored to Ewen of Argyll, finally became part of Scotland.

The Legacy of Somerled

Somerled has achieved a near-mythical reputation: in histories of Clan Donald he is credited with great feats of valour and celebrated as the Celtic hero who drove the Scandinavians out of Argyll. His later life is reasonably documented but his origins are fairly obscure. In spite of this, there are many and varied accounts of his genealogy, with a growing consensus that he was a member of the Gall-Gaedhil: his father Gillebride (Servant of Brigid) and grandfather Gilledomnan (Servant of Adomnan) had Gaelic names, whereas his first name (translated as 'Summer Viking') is clearly Scandinavian, possibly indicating a Norse mother. All of this speculation has now been given further encouragement by a genetic study of the leading families of his descendants (Clan Donald and other clans of the area), which shows that not only do they all carry the typical Norse Y-chromosome (indicating descent from a male Scandinavian) but that they all have a unique mutation that can be dated back to around the time of Somerled. This evidence, that Somerled's father was either Norse or Gall-Gaedhil, need not be inconsistent with his Gaelic name because it was not uncommon for Norse converts to Christianity to adopt the name of a Celtic saint.

Whether Celtic or Norse, Somerled certainly made an impact on the people of Argyll, and it is estimated that he has half a million living descendants worldwide. Reliable genealogical data (confirmed by the genetic study) shows that, via the three MacSorleys, he is the progenitor, through the male line, of many of the leading families in Argyll and surrounding areas: MacDougall, MacDonnell of Islay, Clanranald, MacDonald of Sleat, Macdonell of Keppoch, MacDonnell of Glengarry, MacIan of Ardnamurchan, and MacAllister of Loup (Kintyre). What is particularly interesting is that the presence of the Y-chromosome mutation in nearly all of the current clan chiefs shows that all of the intervening wives have been faithful to their husbands – at least in the production of the heir. Through the female line, he is the ancestor of MacNeil of Barra, MacLean of Duart, and Cameron of Locheil. The other major group of families in Argyll, predominantly in Cowal (Lamont, MacSween, MacEwen, MacLachlan, Macleay – the last converting to Livingstone on Lismore, as explained in Chapter 8) claim a more tenuous and more Celtic descent from Anrothan, a Uí Néill king in Northern Ireland in the eleventh century; but at least two of these names (MacSween – Son of Sweyn; MacLachlan – Son of the Norwegian) reveal a Gall-Gaedhil origin. The outsiders who came to dominate the area, the Campbells, claim to be of British origin, but even the Campbells of Argyll and the Campbells of Glenorchy/ Breadalbane have not been able to avoid being descendants of Somerled through the female line.

Bibliography

McDonald, R.A. (1997) *The Kingdom of the Isles: Scotland's Western Seaboard, c. 1100–c. 1336*. Edinburgh: Tuckwell Press.

Marsden, J. (2000) *Somerled and the Emergence of Gaelic Scotland*. Edinburgh: Tuckwell Press.

Moncreiffe, I. (1967) *The Highland Clans*. London: Barrie & Rockcliffe.

Pálsson, H. and Edwards, P. (trans.) (1981) *Orkneyinga Saga*. London: Penguin.

Sykes, B. (2003) *Adam's Curse: A Future without Men*. London: Bantam.

'Clan Donald USA Genetic Genealogy Project' at http://dna-project. clan-donald-usa.org/dnamain3.htm.

6

Into the Campbell Empire

Later chroniclers looked back to the thirteenth century with nostalgia, recalling a golden age when King Alexander III ruled firmly and wisely, and there were decades of peace with Scotland's neighbours. Their views were coloured by the nightmarish events of the following century, whose horrors match any other period in the history of Europe.

The untimely death of Alexander III in 1286 and the subsequent death of his sole direct heir precipitated Scotland into 20 years of conflict with England and civil war among the different factions. The War of Independence was hardly over, with the decisive battle of Bannockburn in 1314, when northern Europe was overtaken by a sudden deterioration in its weather. Cooler temperatures and heavy rainfall throughout the summer resulted in widespread crop failures. Most of the people of Scotland were subsistence farmers, well able to endure occasional bad seasons, but, this time, the adverse conditions lasted for six years and across Europe death rates rose sharply. The worst of the famine years were over by 1322 but the stable warm conditions of the previous century did not return. The Little Ice Age had begun, bringing generally lower temperatures, greater variation in the weather, and reduced security in the food supply.

After the death of Robert I (The Bruce) in 1329 and the succession of his infant son David II, the country was plunged back into a long period of political insecurity when the rights of the Balliol family were revived by invasion from England and leading families, such as the Stewarts and Douglases, took the opportunity to develop strong independent fiefdoms. As we shall see, the power vacuum also provided opportunities for West Highland leaders. In 1346 David had barely reached manhood when he unwisely invaded England and was defeated and captured at Neville's Cross; he spent the next 11 years imprisoned by the English king. This may have saved his life because, immured in the Tower of London, he was isolated from the Black Death which spread through England in 1349, killing a quarter to a third of the entire population. It reached Scotland by 1350 and, although there are no accurate accounts of mortality, the death toll is unlikely to have been less than in England. The eventual return of David in 1357 was a mixed blessing for the country because the continuing liability for heavy ransom payments crippled the national economy.

Over most of the century, the ordinary people of Scotland were ravaged by successive invading armies, caught in the crossfire of civil war, pressed into service in war galley or armed band, starved by crop failure, and their numbers and vitality reduced unmercifully by disease. It seems a miracle that any structures of society survived. As graphically described by Sigrid Undset in her epic novel *Kristin Lavransdatter*, a parallel combination of events in the fourteenth century destroyed both the power and organisation of Norway, leaving the way clear for Denmark to dominate Scandinavia. The early decades of the fifteenth century in Scotland were little better, with continual feuding between powerful families, and a line of Stewart kings handicapped by early deaths and unwise policies. In the west, out of this turmoil, the Campbells and MacDonalds rose to power at the expense of the MacDougalls.

The Eclipse of the MacDougalls

After the Treaty of Perth (1266), Ewen MacDougall, Lord of Argyll, did all he could to adapt to the new world, with Alexander III as sole ruler of the West Highlands and Islands. Apart from naming his heir after the king, he enmeshed his family in a network of marriage alliances with Lowland families. Alexander (or Alasdair) MacDougall was linked with the dominant Comyn faction by his marriage to a daughter of John, Lord of Badenoch and Lochaber. Other Comyn daughters were wives of prominent

Norman knights, and their brother, John, married Eleanor, sister of the future King John Balliol. Another strand of the network involved the marriage of Alexander's sister Mary to the Earl of Strathearn. The only notable marriage out of line with this policy was that, sometime around 1290, between Alexander MacDonald of Islay and Juliana MacDougall. This was of great importance to Lismore because her dowry, disputed for many years, included land on the island.

During the second half of the thirteenth century the MacDougalls were one of four principal families in the West Highlands: the powerful Stewarts, with extensive lands in Cowal as well as Menteith, soon to provide Kings of Scots on the failure of the Bruce line; the up-and-coming Campbells, extending north, east and west from the area around Loch Awe and north Cowal; the MacDonalds in Islay and Kintyre; and the MacDougalls, who laid claim to much of Ardnamurchan, Morvern, Duror, Glencoe, Lochaber, Mull and Tiree, as well as Lorn, including Benderloch, Appin and Lismore. In this period, the MacDougalls were well able to hold their own against the ambitions of their MacDonald and Campbell neighbours.

The power and wealth of the MacDougalls can be seen in their extraordinary investment in the new style of stone fortresses during the first half of the thirteenth century. Apart from the main castle at Dunstaffnage, there were substantial fortified structures in MacDougall territory at Dunollie near Oban, at Duart and Aros on Mull, and at Ardtornish on the other shore of the Sound of Mull in Morvern. There are two castles from this period on spectacular coastal sites on Lismore at Achinduin and Coeffin, in sight of one another and commanding the western approaches to the island. Achinduin (Plate 11a) is typical of the major castles of the area and period, with massive masonry walls, up to 2.5m thick, enclosing an area of around 22m square. Within the enclosure are the remains of substantial living quarters and, in the best-preserved north-west curtain wall, a gateway leads directly to a stair which gave access to the ramparts. The castle makes good use of the natural defence offered by a steep ridge of limestone, commanding extensive views to the west. Its line of sight to Duart forms a link with the three contemporary castles in the Sound of Mull.

The remains at Coeffin (Plate 11b) are less substantial. The original structure appears to have been a relatively modest hall house, around 13m × 5m internally, with very thick walls (between 1.5m and 2m). A stair in the north corner, now ruined, gave access to the upper floor and the ramparts. The hall occupies the whole of a narrow ridge overlooking the bay, and it is protected all round by steep slopes. An outer enclosure, which may be of a later date, covered the main entrance on the north-east wall.

These are large and enduring structures, built with care. The main fabrics are local materials – limestone rubble with prominent red and grey granite boulders – and there is extensive use of lime mortar with coarse gravel in the infilling of the walls, much of which remains durable after more than 700 years. It must have required enormous amounts of charcoal to fire clamp kilns on the island. The use of a professional stonemason, who appears to have also played a part in the early stages of the construction of the cathedral, is confirmed by his marks on a lintel at Achinduin.

Little is known about the building and occupation of Achinduin and Coeffin Castles in the thirteenth and fourteenth centuries, although there is archaeological evidence of beach clearance for the hauling up of boats, and nearby fishtraps may date back to medieval times (Plate 11b). Excavation of Achinduin in the 1970s revealed a range of objects from the medieval period (Plate 8a). Because Achinduin was used by the Bishop of Argyll in the fifteenth century, it has generally been assumed that it was built specifically for the bishopric. However, documents of the period, and the poverty of the diocese, suggest that it was primarily a stronghold of the MacDougalls, built to secure their ownership of Lismore, but it is not clear why they needed two highly fortified castles on the same island. One recent idea is that, in a period of very active building in stone of castles and religious houses, they protected the only source of lime on the western seaboard.

In 1295 Alexander MacDougall must have been satisfied with the outcome of the political strategies of his family over 30 years. As part of the powerful Comyn faction, he was one of the 40 'auditors' supporting John Balliol over the other claimants to the Scottish throne, including the Bruces. The reward from the successful Balliol was appointment as the first sheriff of Lorn, including Lismore, with authority to keep the peace in the Western Isles. The regional balance of power was shifted towards the MacDougalls and away from the Campbells and MacDonalds of Islay, both supporters of the Bruce cause. Hostility between MacDougall and MacDonald intensified when King John intervened in the Lismore dowry dispute, taking the island into his own possession. Illustrating the great complexity of the relationships of the time, Edward I then ordered Balliol to appear before him in England to answer for withholding part of Lismore from Alexander of Islay and Juliana, his wife.

This was to be a short-lived triumph for Alexander. Edward I of England soon became impatient with the policies of his chosen King of Scots and invaded Scotland in 1296 to take control. After a brief and unsuccessful attempt to challenge Edward in the field of battle, the Comyns capitulated and King John was deposed. Instead of installing the second claimant in line, now Robert Bruce the Younger, he undertook a royal progress through the east and north-east of Scotland, demanding the submission, in person, of all major landowners. Alexander MacDougall travelled to Elgin to submit but, because his son Duncan did not also do so, Edward imprisoned Alexander at Berwick, and commissioned Alexander Stewart, Earl of Menteith, to occupy Argyll with the assistance of Colin Campbell of Loch Awe and Alexander of Islay. This alliance seems to have been singularly ineffectual because, shortly afterwards, Campbell was killed in a skirmish with the MacDougalls, and Alexander of Islay died under suspicious circumstances.

Meanwhile, around 1297 and 1298, the only effective opposition to Edward was offered by William Wallace and Andrew Moray, who won a startling victory at Stirling Bridge but eventually, owing to the inability of the different Scottish factions to cooperate, lost at Falkirk. During the following years, Edward's armies marched through south-west and eastern Scotland, securing the submission of most of the landowners, occupying their castles, and obliging many of them to provide military service at home and in Flanders. In 1301 Alexander was freed from imprisonment when his sons finally submitted to the English king. Sir Neil Campbell followed in 1302.

Although the Bruces did not accept the validity of Edward's judgement and were opposed to the Comyn–Balliol alliance, they behaved in a way that seems now to be erratic. This was at least partly because they were major landowners in England and, therefore, already Edward's feudal vassals. For example, in 1298

Robert Bruce the Elder fought on Edward's side against his own son at the Battle of Falkirk. Later, the Younger campaigned on Edward's side in 1303 and took his place amongst the Guardians of Scotland. An uncertain peace was established around 1304–5, by which time virtually all the major landowners had submitted to Edward.

All of this was to change on 12 February 1306 when Robert Bruce, now Earl of Carrick, and potentially one of the richest men *in England*, on the death of his father, murdered John Comyn, Lord of Badenoch, in Greyfriars Church at Dumfries. With nothing now to lose, he raised a rebellion in the south-west and quickly mustered enough support for his coronation as King of Scots at Scone on 25 March. The English army, under Aymer de Valence, was soon in pursuit, inflicting a major defeat at Methven on 19 June. Bruce's depleted forces were driven west along Loch Tay, eventually colliding with the men of Argyll under John MacDougall, son of Alexander, at Dailrigh near Tyndrum. Bruce narrowly escaped from this second defeat, but left behind the famous Brooch of Lorn which is still the prized possession of the MacDougalls. The course of Scottish history could well have been entirely different if Bruce had been captured or killed.

Again, this was only a temporary reprieve for the MacDougalls. As a fugitive in the west in the winter of 1306–7, Bruce was supported by the Campbells (Sir Neil Campbell, a long-term supporter, was an 'auditor' of the Bruces and possibly a kinsman), and Clan Donald. He was eventually delivered, in spring 1307, to his own lands in Carrick, Ayrshire. There followed a guerrilla campaign in the south-west, carried into the Comyn heartland of the north-east from September, sapping the strength of the occupying forces by winning small battles and systematically reducing their strongholds. The castle of Inverlochy, stronghold of the Lord of Badenoch and Lochaber, fell to his forces by November. With Edward I dying at the English border in July 1307, his son Edward II failing to provide consistent opposition, and the Stewarts switching allegiance, Bruce was sufficiently secure by summer 1308 to take his revenge on the MacDougalls. He defeated them at the Pass of Brander in August and moved on to besiege and capture the castle of Dunstaffnage with the assistance of the MacDonalds in October.

The defeated MacDougalls, Alexander and his son John, fled into exile and, becoming pensioners of the King of England, they were involved in military and naval action against King Robert in Ireland and the north of England. Both had died by 1316 but John's son Allan continued to serve in the household of Edward II. Their lands were forfeited and distributed mainly among the Campbells and MacDonalds, who had proved consistent supporters of the Bruce claim. Clan Donald, in particular, had distinguished themselves on the field of Bannockburn. In redistributing and confirming the possession of much of the landholding in the west, King Robert formalised the legal position: possession was directly from the crown, on condition that the landholder provided boat service (12- to 20-oared birlinns, each with a fully-armed crew of three men per oar), rather than the conventional knights-at-arms, when required by the king. In his fugitive months, Bruce had learned the value of amphibious operations.

The crown claimed the important fortress at Dunstaffnage, but most of Lorn was parcelled up into smaller baronies and entrusted to Sir Arthur Campbell, Captain of Dunstaffnage, who belonged to a separate branch of the family from the Campbells of Loch Awe. The 1329 grant of land in Appin was in return for the service of one birlinn of 20 oars with men and provisions. However, it is known that MacDougalls did return to Dunollie before 1329 and, because Lismore is not listed in the lands to be forfeited, it has been suggested that Achinduin Castle provided a refuge for the family in the intervening period. This could explain the 1334 grant of land at Achinduin to the Bishop of Argyll by a landowner identified as Ewen MacDougall.

As a result of these changes, the future of the West Highlands and Islands would now depend upon three leading families: Campbells of Argyll and Glenorchy, MacDonald of Islay, and descendants of Robert the Steward of Scotland. In particular, the transfer of MacDougall lands in Ardnamurchan, Duror, Glencoe, Mull and Tiree, and Comyn lands in Lochaber to Angus Og of Islay was the first step in the rise of the MacDonald Lords of the Isles.

The Lordship of the Isles

With the death of Robert I in 1329, Scotland was, once again, plunged into chaos. In the pursuit of peaceful relations across the border, in 1328, his four-year-old son David had been married to Joan, sister of Edward III, but this did not prevent the English king from supporting the claim of the Balliol family against the new king, David II. After two crushing defeats of the Scots by English armies, Edward Balliol was also crowned King of Scots in 1332. The young King David and his queen, protected by the Stewarts in Dumbarton Castle, were eventually sent to France in 1334 for safekeeping, and did not return to Scotland until 1341. The start of the Hundred Years' War with France soon diverted Edward III from active involvement in Scottish affairs, leaving Robert Stewart (the future Robert II) as Guardian, to dominate for much of David's minority.

These developments were broadly favourable to the ruling families in the west. The solidarity between Campbells and Stewarts allowed the former quietly to consolidate their position around Loch Awe while the MacDonalds of Islay, opting to support Balliol in the early 1330s, took the opportunity of the general confusion to strengthen their position by force. By 1336 John of Islay was styling himself 'Lord of the Isles', a new title of his own making, with no legal foundation. His boldness paid off when, on making peace with the returning king, his occupation of Knapdale, Gigha, Colonsay, Mull, Morvern and Lochaber was confirmed, and the extinction of the MacRuairis in 1346 brought Garmoran into the possession of Clan Donald. This new lordship of the Isles, extending from Morvern to Knoydart and including all of the islands from Islay to Rum and the Uists, was approaching the extent of Somerled's empire. In a development that would have great importance for the future of the area, Lord John encouraged the Macleans to occupy the lands on Mull vacated by the MacDougalls.

David II and the Return of John (Gallda) MacDougall

In 1346, five years after his return from France, but still only 23, David II invaded England and suffered a major defeat at Neville's Cross. Captured on the field of battle, he was imprisoned for 11 years by his brother-in-law Edward III, who was not prepared to enter into reasonable negotiations about ransom payments. As a result, between his childhood in France, and his imprisonment in London, David spent a total of 33 years of his reign outside Scotland.

In his absence, Robert Stewart resumed control, but the politics of the west were changing. The continuing advance of the MacDonalds, now penetrating into Moray and encroaching on the earldom of Ross, went unchallenged by Stewart. On the contrary, he became the father-in-law of John, Lord of the Isles, in 1350, and part of the marriage settlement seems to have been the return of Kintyre to the MacDonalds. Meanwhile, as the Stewarts' focus moved eastwards, Gillespic Campbell of Loch Awe was granted much of the land they vacated in Cowal and Knapdale.

An accident of history brought the prisoner, King David, into contact with John MacDougall, known as Gallda, the foreigner, because he was raised in England, where his father was a member of Edward's household. They became firm friends: John Gallda married David's niece, Joanna Bruce, and when David returned to Scotland in 1357 he gave the ancestral MacDougall lands in Lorn back to John. This curbing of the ambitions of the MacArthur Campbells to dominate the western seaboard may, in fact, have been a recognition that it had proved impossible to loosen the hold of the MacDougalls on the area, but the islands, except Lismore, remained with the MacDonalds.

Again, the MacDougalls were fated to lose the lordship of Lorn, this time for the last time. John Gallda had two legitimate daughters, who married brothers John and Robert of a cadet branch of the Stewart family (of Innermeath in Perthshire), and at least one illegitimate son, Allan MacDougall. At the death of Gallda in the 1370s, Allan challenged for the inheritance but by 1388 Robert Stewart and his wife had formally resigned Lorn, Benderloch, Appin and Lismore to John Stewart. He assumed the title of Lord of Lorn, with the MacDougalls of Dunolllie acting as baillies and retaining the ancient right to foster the heir to the lordship. The overall effect of these developments was that the Campbells of Loch Awe, now the most powerful family on the western mainland, began to style themselves Lords of Argyll.

Seeds of Conflict: Campbell, Stewart and MacDonald

The uneasy relationship between the Stewarts of Appin and the Campbells, which even played a part in the infamous Appin murder

400 years later (Chapter 9), had its origin in the inability of the Stewart Lords of Lorn to maintain continuity of the male line. As the successful claimants to the lordship, the Argyll Campbells laid the foundations of their reputation for ruthlessness and deviousness, but it is also difficult to admire the behaviour of the Stewarts.

By the 1430s, the Campbell interest was shared by the main Argyll line, and a major cadet branch, the Campbells of Glenorchy, whose expansion eastwards into Perthshire would give rise to a dynasty, the Earls of Breadalbane, which rivalled the power of the Argylls. In the reigns of James I and II, the Campbells acted closely with the Stewart Lords of Lorn to limit the ambitions of the Lords of the Isles, who posed a major threat to the crown. This alliance was cemented by the marriages of two of John of Lorn's daughters: Janet Stewart to Colin Campbell of Glenorchy and Isabella Stewart to Colin Campbell (1st Earl of Argyll from 1458).

By 1460, John Stewart, Lord of Lorn, without a legitimate male heir, had drawn up a legal entail to ensure that his brother Walter, rather than his daughters, would inherit. Walter, however, was aware of two major challengers: Dugald Stewart, John's illegitimate son (the progenitor of the Stewarts of Appin), and Allan MacDougall, who had ambitions to overthrow the leaders of Clan MacDougall, within Lorn, with the help of MacDonald of Islay. In a tight situation, the Stewarts asked for assistance from the Earl of Argyll, who rescued the Chief of MacDougall from imprisonment on Kerrera, but his condition for supporting Walter against Dugald was a share of the lands of Lorn when he inherited.

The situation rapidly became more complicated. In 1462 Allan MacDougall captured Dunstaffnage and killed John of Lorn, who was apparently on the point of marrying to legitimise his son Dugald (MacDougall historians claim that the marriage was completed before he died). Walter inherited the lordship but, being unable to control events, his authority was undermined by Dugald Stewart. He also reneged on his promise to share his inheritance with Argyll. At this point, as on other occasions, the Campbells of Argyll and Glenorchy resorted to the courts rather than the sword and, after a lengthy process, Argyll gained possession of his father-in-law's lordship in 1470, with one-third of the land awarded to Glenorchy in recognition of Janet Stewart's claim. Walter Stewart departed to the prospect of a more peaceful life on land exchanged with the Campbells in the east of Scotland.

The Campbells had now reached the west coast, at a critical time in the politics of the west. After a long struggle over many decades between the crown and Clan Donald, including the indecisive Battle of Harlaw in 1411 and the crushing victory over the royal army at Inverlochy in 1431, Alexander, 3rd Lord of the Isles, was able to expand the lordship in 1439 to include the earldom of Ross. The centre of power in the lordship moved into Ross, the warlike MacDonalds of Dunivaig in Islay took control in the south, and a lasting pattern of powerful cadets and client groups began to emerge: Macleans in Mull and Morvern; MacNeils on Barra; Clanranald in the old Garmoran lands; MacIans in Ardnamurchan; MacLeods in Skye and Lewis. With the Earls of Argyll increasingly trusted with the administration of the kingdom, and the Lords of the Isles viewing themselves as semi-independent rulers able to negotiate directly with the English crown, the scene was being set for serious conflict.

Lismore, shared between Argyll and Glenorchy, with a portion being returned to the Stewarts of Appin, was again in a frontier zone at the leading edge of the Campbell advance. To the west they faced the ever-present risk of raiding parties of Macleans from Mull and Morvern, MacIans from Ardnamurchan, and MacDonalds from Islay. In Lorn, in spite of carrying judicial authority, Campbell peace was threatened by the presence of discontented groups of MacDougalls and Stewarts. As we shall see in the next chapter, the long-term strategy of the Campbells was a progressive leasing of the land to loyal tacksmen under the supervision of factors drawn from cadet families such as the Campbells of Barcaldine, acting for Glenorchy. Much of their success lay in the continuing coherence of Clan Campbell – a lesson that the Lords of the Isles failed to learn.

The Bishopric of Argyll

The building of the cathedral on Lismore seems to have been completed by the middle of the fourteenth century, possibly under Bishop Martin (1342–62), but, in the absence of early MacDougall

Sanctuary Stone

FIGURE 6.1   Pictorial reconstruction of the completed cathedral on Lismore
during the first half of the fourteenth century, showing the Sanctuary Stone
in the foreground and Cnoc Aingeal in the distance (reproduced with the
permission of Donald Black).

documents, little is known about the financing, planning, or
architectural details of the project, or even of the source and delivery
of the dressed sandstone used in parts of the building. The present
parish church is accommodated within the walls of the cathedral
choir, reduced from their original height by up to 3m in 1749, but
because of plastering inside and harling outside there are very few
visible traces of the original building. All that can be seen are seven
external buttresses identified as typical of Decorated Gothic style
(correct for the building period), and two round-headed doorways
in the south and west walls (now closed). As the orientation of
the building was reversed in a major renovation in 1900, the well-
preserved sedilia (three stone seats to accommodate the priests
celebrating mass) and piscina (where chalices could be washed),
which were near the original altar at the east end, are now near the
entrance to the modern church.

Nothing remains of the nave above ground, but excavations
in the 1950s showed that the overall internal dimensions of the
building were 38m x 7.2m, the nave being 21m long and of the
same width as the choir. There was a small square tower at the west

end enclosing an area of 2.5m × 2.5m, and traces of a chapel have been found outside the north wall of the choir. The walls of the nave were mainly limestone and whinstone rubble, but most of the stone had been removed with the dressed sandstone, probably from Morvern, used to build the church manse in the eighteenth century. There was a general lack of stone carving. Compared with other contemporary cathedrals in Scotland, this was a very modest, plain and simple structure. The nearest example is probably Dornoch (length 38m, choir width 7m) but here, before nineteenth-century remodelling, the nave had north and south aisles, which increased the width to 18m. Whether through poor building or neglect, the Lismore cathedral was already said by James IV to be in ruins by 1512.

The modesty of the building is consistent with the level of funding of the diocese and it is likely that the suspension of Bishop Martin from his post, for attempting to divert church revenues, was a result of his commitment to completing the building programme. From the reign of David I, the primary source of funding for the church was through taxation of the production of each parish: the teind or tenth part. This posed problems for the diocese because of the relatively low productivity of the land in Argyll and the fact that, in a turbulent era, securing the teinds could prove difficult. Furthermore, although they were supposed to support the parish vicar, his church building and manse, and his charitable work, the teinds were increasingly diverted ('annexed') to other religious foundations, some not even in the area. The bishopric of Argyll participated in this diversion of funding, for example being granted the revenues of Kilbride (Oban) by Alexander II in 1249, but it drew funds from only a few adjacent parishes because so many had been pre-empted by others: six to the collegiate church of Kilmun; five to Ardchattan Priory; four to Paisley Abbey; three to Iona Abbey; two to Inchaffrey Abbey (Perthshire); and one each to Kilwinning Abbey and Fail Priory (both Ayrshire). The inevitable result of this appropriation of funds was a general shortage of educated vicars, the uniting of parishes, and sub-standard churches and manses.

Larger religious institutions also attracted endowments from landowners, normally in the form of grants of land from which they drew rent and produce, but also cash, silver and gold plate, and jewellery. It is surprising that the diocese of Argyll did not receive a 'dowry' of endowments from its parent, Dunkeld. However, much of the south-west quarter of Lismore was set aside by the MacDougalls for the support of the cathedral. In 1241 Ewen of Argyll granted to William, Bishop of Argyll, 14 pennylands in Lismore, some areas of which can still be identified: 'Barnaray [Bernera]; 2.5 pennylands of Achacendune [Achinduin]; 5 of Tyrchulen; 2 of Tyrknannen; 1.5 of Tenga; one of Drumchulochir; and one of Craganas [Craignich].' In 1304 the MacDougalls extended the area by granting Bishop Andrew 5.5 pennylands near Achinduin (Pennyngscanhach, Tyrfeirlach, Achychnahunsen and Geyle). A later document (1334) suggests that the area covered the townships of Achinduin, Frackersaig and Craignich. These arrangements continued until 1507, when they were confirmed by James IV, and the very modest endowments of the now defunct Saddell Abbey (amounting to £9 sterling) transferred to Lismore.

There were other sources of funding. For example, in 1506 James IV granted to David, Bishop of Argyll, all of the fines to be exacted in the forthcoming round of law courts (justice ayres) in Argyll, Lorn and Cowal. Nevertheless, it is clear that the bishopric and the parishes within the diocese were chronically handicapped by inadequate finances and, on at least one occasion (1411), the bishop was obliged to appeal directly to the Pope for support. A thirteenth-century audit gave the following annual incomes for Scottish dioceses: St Andrews £8,018; Glasgow £4,080; Aberdeen £1,610; Moray £1,418; Dunkeld £1,206; Dunblane £507; Brechin £416; Galloway £358; Ross £351; Dornoch £286; Argyll £281.

Apart from financial problems, there were other obstacles to maintaining a full complement of Gaelic-speaking clergy, including continuing political insecurity, the commercial and spiritual impact of plague from 1350, and the relative isolation of the new cathedral. Under Church protocol, each bishop was elected by a full chapter, including, at the minimum:

Dean – the senior administrator, with additional legal responsibilities

Treasurer – manager of the Cathedral property

Chancellor – responsible for correspondence, library and education

Precentor – responsible for ritual and music

Archdeacon – the spiritual deputy of the bishop

and varying numbers of ordinary priests or prebendaries. In the case of Argyll, there were, at different times, Deans of Kintyre, Glassary, Lorn and Morvern, representing the bishop in these areas. A full chapter was certainly not established before 1250 and the surviving records indicate that vacancies were common. Some posts may have been non-resident. For example, the precentor was, for some time, provided from the clergy at Ardchattan.

At times, the life of the diocese was dominated by local and national politics. At least two of the early bishops were MacDougalls (Laurence of Argyll, 1264–99; Martin of Argyll, 1342–62) and, when Alexander MacDougall was driven into exile in 1308, Bishop Andrew (1300–27) followed him to England with direct financial support from Edward II. As a result, the diocese lacked a spiritual leader for nearly 20 years. A later incumbent, Bishop Finlay (1420–6), was directly involved in an armed uprising against James I and fled to Ireland when it failed in 1425. As we shall see in Chapter 8, in the sixteenth and seventeenth centuries the Campbell landlords continued to use members of the clergy as lawyers and witnesses in their legal transactions and they were influential in securing posts for their vassals, including illegitimate sons of priests.

Another important theme in the early years was the influence of the preaching order of the Dominicans, often referred to as the shock troops of Christian orthodoxy against heresy, who were entrusted with operating the Inquisition from 1233. The order provided four bishops (Laurence of Argyll, Andrew, Martin of Argyll and Finlay). The initiator of this link was probably Bishop Clement of Dunblane, who presided over the vacancy after Bishop William was drowned in 1241. Although the Blackfriars were normally associated with renewal of the Church in towns in Scotland (there were strong communities in Ayr, Glasgow, Perth and Stirling and they exerted political leverage on the king and his influential courtiers such as the Earls of Argyll), the Church may have seen the outlying Gaelic-speaking areas of Scotland as an important mission field.

The need to fill the vacancy caused by the flight of Finlay in 1425 introduced an issue that was to become only too familiar in subsequent years. Whether or not the Lowlander George Lauder of Balcomie in Fife, previously vicar of Crail (bishop 1427–61), was a Gaelic speaker, he certainly began to introduce priests without fluency in the language to parishes in the diocese. This brought him into direct conflict with the Campbells, who were moving towards becoming the dominant influence in Argyll, providing two long-serving archdeacons during this period. Eventually, the issue reached the very highest courts. The case against Lowland parish priests was presented to the Pope in 1466 by Colin Campbell of Glenorchy, James III's ambassador in Rome. Although there was agreement that, in line with one of the original motives for the establishment of the diocese, parish priests in Argyll had to be fluent in Gaelic, this was the beginning of the dilution of the language. All subsequent bishops were Lowlanders.

Monumental Sculpture

The collection of around 15 late medieval carved gravestones associated with the cathedral on Lismore is modest compared with those on Iona and Oronsay, or at Kilmartin and Keil in Morvern, but some are unique. Most were carved in the fourteenth or fifteenth century, in the MacDougall and Stewart eras, and, because the Lismore limestone was unsuitable, they would generally have been created elsewhere from the hard but cleaving Loch Sween chlorite schist. Five have been attributed to the Iona School, two to the Lochawe School, and five others to less skilful craftsmen.

The finest of the Iona stones, lying flat in the graveyard near the east end of the church (Plate 12a) features a Viking-style sword, complex plant scrolls and two mythical beasts. However, two plainer Iona stones, one set into the floor of the church, one a fragment housed in the museum, display 'Tau-headed staves' (Plate 10) – unique in Scotland but common as ecclesiastical decorations in the Eastern Orthodox Church. No satisfactory explanation has

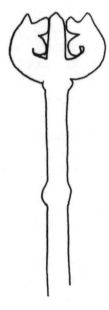

FIGURE 6.2   Tracing of the Tau symbol in Plate 10

been advanced to explain these decorations, although the church stone may commemorate one or more precentors of the cathedral who carried a stave as their badge of office. One speculation is that the symbol could have been brought back by a crusader knight. Later, the larger stone was reused for the burial of the murdered Duncan Stewart of Appin in 1519 (Chapter 7).

One of the cruder stones in the graveyard, unusually, has an image of a woman, still reasonably distinct. The description in the RCAHMS inventory reads: 'Within a niche at the top of the stone there is a small figure of a woman, facing the front and with arms akimbo. She is wearing a close-fitting hood, and an ankle length kirtle over which is an outer garment, possibly a cote-hardie, with long flaps (tippets) hanging from the elbows.' We do not know who this wealthy lady was, with her tight-fitting dress and flowing hem, and there are no inscriptions on the other stones. However, a fine sixteenth-century tomb chest lid, with sword, plant scrolls and mythical creatures (Plate 12b), to the north of the church, is known to mark the grave of Donald Stewart of Invernahyle (Chapter 8). Later than the Iona and Lochawe Schools, it is very similar to chest lids at Kilmichael Glassary, but the accompanying stone (Plate 12b), said to commemorate Stewart's Carmichael armour- bearer, appears to be of earlier date.

Bibliography

Boardman, S. (2006) *The Campbells, 1250–1513*. Edinburgh: John Donald.

Brown, A.L. and Duncan, A.A.M. (1957) 'The Cathedral Church of Lismore.' *Transactions of the Scottish Ecclesiological Society* 15: 41–50.

Campbell, A. (2000) *A History of Clan Campbell: 1. From Origins to Flodden*. Edinburgh: Polygon.

Paterson, R.C. (2001) *The Lords of the Isles*. Edinburgh: Birlinn.

Steer, K.A. and Bannerman, J.W.M. (1977) *Late Medieval Monumental Sculpture in the West Highlands*. Edinburgh: HMSO.

Turner, D. (1998) 'The Bishops of Argyll and the Castle of Achanduin, Lismore, AD.' *Proceedings of the Society of Antiquaries of Scotland* 128: 645–52.

Watt, D.E.R. and Murray, A.L. (2003) *Fasti Ecclesiae Scoticanae Medii Aevi ad Annum 1638*. Edinburgh: Scottish Records Society.

7

The Glenorchy Years

Colin Campbell, 1st Earl of Argyll, was politically very adept in his relations with the crown. Favoured by James II, he was prominent in the government of James III, but eventually joined the leaders of the rebellion that led to the violent death of the king in 1488. Almost immediately he assumed the chancellorship of Scotland under the new king, James IV, overseeing a major readjustment of landholding across the country. This included the return of part of Campbell-held Lorn (Appin and part of northern Lismore) to the Stewarts of Appin, but it also saw a major expansion of the influence of the Campbells of Glenorchy around Loch Tay.

Within a few years (1508), the Stewarts had sold a substantial part of their portion of the island (Killandrist, Portcharron and Kinlochan) back to Archibald, 2nd Earl of Argyll, and, thereafter, the story of Lismore is dominated by Argyll and Glenorchy up to 1734, when the Glenorchy family (now Earls of Breadalbane) transferred their holding to the Campbells of Barcaldine. The early eighteenth century is, therefore, an important time in the history of Lismore because of the break-up of the island into smaller parcels. By the 1751 valuation (Table, page 114) there were nine different proprietors of land on the island, in addition to the Livingstones of Bachuil, but none resident. This was an important factor in the later clearance of people from parts of the island.

Even though the Argyll Campbells owned a large part of Lismore over this period and are, indeed, still landowners on the island, this chapter refers to the 'Glenorchy Years'. While the Earls

73

of Argyll were deeply involved in affairs of state, the Lords of Glenorchy were focused on the expansion and consolidation of their estates, which eventually extended from Lorn to the east end of Loch Tay, incorporating productive lands in Perthshire as well as wilder areas in Glenlyon and Achallader, on the fringes of Rannoch Moor. 'Grey Colin', who, as Lord of Glenorchy from 1550 to 1583 steered his way successfully through the troubled waters of the Reformation years (Chapter 8), was so taken up with his continuing feud with his former allies, the MacGregors of Glenstrae, that he declined to submit in person to Queen Mary in 1565. He escaped disaster by deploying the diplomatic skills of his wife Katherine Ruthven.

Both Argyll and Glenorchy relied on the MacDougalls of Dunollie to look after their affairs in Lorn and Lismore and, although their relationship was complex, Glenorchy also called upon the Stewarts of Appin from time to time. These arrangements changed under the 7th Lord of Glenorchy, Sir Duncan Campbell (1545–1631), otherwise known as Black Duncan, who built the strong tower house of Barcaldine (the 'Black Castle' – at that time not harled) in the early years of the seventeenth century and installed a branch of the family, the Campbells of Invergeldie (later known as the Campbells of Barcaldine), to be his factors in the area. Black Duncan was totally ruthless and treacherous in his relationships with both kinsmen and neighbours, but he was also a very early Improver, obliging his tenants to adopt more efficient husbandry. As he and his father were also avid record-keepers, the Black Book of Taymouth and other records preserved in the Breadalbane and Barcaldine papers provide an unparalleled insight into their lands on Lismore. What we know about life on the island is largely drawn from detailed studies of these documents and there is a need to redress the balance with more studies of relevant documents in the Argyll archives. However, before looking at the local and domestic aspects of Lismore in the sixteenth and seventeenth centuries, it is necessary to establish the historical context of these centuries and how the Campbells controlled, but also protected, their interests in difficult times. The events surrounding the Reformation in Scotland, and how they affected Lismore and the diocese of Argyll, are considered in Chapter 8.

The Extinction of the Lordship of the Isles

By the 1440s, the Lords of the Isles were at their most powerful, controlling the Hebrides, Kintyre, Morvern, the MacIain and Clanranald lands from Ardnamurchan north, and the extensive earldom of Ross. In 1460, when England was tearing itself apart in the Wars of the Roses, and Scotland had a new nine-year-old king, John, Lord of the Isles, saw an opportunity to extend his power. In October 1461, in an alliance with the exiled Earl of Douglas, John entered into negotiations in Morvern with envoys from Edward IV and the agreement was formalised in London in February 1462, under the grandiose title of the Treaty of Westminster–Ardtornish. John was to become the liegeman of Edward and receive a substantial financial subsidy from England in peace and war. With the overthrow of James III, he would be granted all of mainland Scotland north of the Forth, and Douglas would reclaim his wide estates in the south.

In dealing directly with England, John was following a pattern of behaviour common to powerful MacSorleys in earlier centuries, but he failed to learn the lessons of history. Even though the extent of his treason must have been widely known, he was immune from punishment during the minority of James III, submitting formally at Inverness in 1464. By 1475, having dealt with the threat of invasion by Douglas, the king summoned John to answer for his treasonable actions. To the disgust of his clansmen, John's defiance was short-lived, and he surrendered to the authorities in 1476. Possibly calculating that the continuation of the Lordship was necessary to maintain the balance of power in the west, James III stripped John of the earldom of Ross and his lands in Kintyre and Knapdale, but reaffirmed him as Lord of the Isles.

However, this policy, and particularly the loss of the heartland of Kintyre, did not take into account the pride of Clan Donald. Angus Og, the illegitimate son of John, but legitimised and married to a daughter of the Earl of Argyll, rose in rebellion in 1481, rallying the MacDonalds of Islay, Clanranald, Lochalsh and Sleat. Only the subsidiary clans (Maclean, MacNeil and MacLeod) remained loyal to John, and their fleet of birlinns was soundly beaten at the Battle of Bloody Bay on the north-east coast of Mull, leaving the way clear for Angus to assume the role of Lord of the Isles. Although he

succeeded in reoccupying Ross by force, his reign was short as he
was assassinated around 1490. Alexander MacDonald of Lochalsh
assumed the leadership of the MacDonalds briefly, but the lordship
of the Isles was finally wound up when the young James IV lost
patience in 1493. John re-emerged from obscurity to become a
royal pensioner but, from that time, the individual portions of the
lordship were to be held directly from the king.

Thus began what traditional historians called the *Linn nan
Creach* – normally translated as the Age of Forays. For around
150 years, four successive Lords of the Isles had had some success
in unifying the western seaboard, providing strong personal
leadership and using the Council of the Isles to resolve potential
conflicts and keep the wilder elements under control. This gave the
opportunity for the traditional 'Gaelic learned orders' (specialists
in poetry, history, law, music, medicine, art and fine craftwork) to
flourish, but the greatest achievement is represented by intricately
carved gravestones and crosses. The best of these are to be found
today on Islay, Iona and Oronsay, where the Lordship established
an Augustinian priory, but their influence was wide and can be
traced on gravestones throughout the west, including Lismore
(Chapter 6).

From the late fifteenth century onwards, coherence was lost in
spite of sporadic attempts to reinstate the Lordship. In the absence
of centralised control bloody feuds broke out, most spectacularly
between the MacDonalds of Dunivaig on Islay and the Macleans
of Duart, the dominant Maclean clan controlling more than half
of Mull; and between the MacLeods of Skye and the MacDonalds
of Sleat and Clanranald. Raids and counter-raids continued over
more than two centuries, but the warring factions could still be
united against the common Campbell foe, as in the systematic
destruction of life and property in Argyll by Alasdair MacColla
aided by Macleans, MacDougalls and Lamonts in the 1640s.

Some idea of what life was like during the *Linn nan Creach*
can be gained from traditional accounts of the murder and rescue
of the body of Duncan Stewart of Appin in 1519. On a visit to
Maclean of Duart in search of a reconciliation between their
warring clans, Stewart brought only one follower, Sorley MacColl,
whose sporting prowess during the games arranged for their
entertainment aroused such jealousy that Maclean's men murdered

him. Honour required that Stewart try to avenge the death but, alone and unarmed, he was overpowered and killed and his body hung on the battlements at Duart. One version of the subsequent events tells that when word of the murders reached his close friend MacLeay of Bachuil on Lismore, he felt compelled to rescue Stewart's body for Christian burial. Setting out for Mull in a rowing boat, accompanied by his two red-haired daughters, he succeeded in recovering the body and getting it into the boat but the alarm was raised and the Macleans were soon in pursuit in a four-oared boat. It seemed to be an unequal competition but, by superior seamanship and knowledge of the many rocks and skerries, the baron and his daughters were able to bring the body safely ashore. The alternative version also emphasises the triumph of mind over violence: MacCellaich, a boat builder, rows over to Duart, drills holes in the hulls of the Maclean boats, and conceals them with lard. In this case, the pursuing Macleans are drowned when their boats reach deep water. Such stories could be dismissed as myths were it not that Stewart of Appin is known to have been buried on Lismore under the 'Tau-headed stave' grave slab originally near the altar of the cathedral and now under the stairs near the door of the modern church (Chapter 6).

This cowardly killing of vulnerable individuals was not an isolated event but part of a pattern of uncompromising lawlessness and cruelty. Soon after, in 1527, the Duart chief tired of his wife, a sister of the Earl of Argyll. Some versions of the story claim that she had tried to poison him. He arranged for her to be stranded on Lady Rock, to the south of Lismore, in the expectation that she would be drowned at the next high tide. Rescued by passing fishermen, she was secretly reunited with her family at Inveraray, and when Maclean visited to share his grief with the Campbells, he was confronted by his 'deceased' wife. He did not avoid the vengeance of the Campbells for long.

From time to time, James IV and James V took an active interest in dealing with unrest, undertaking royal cruises to intimidate the ruling clans but generally leaving the thankless work of policing the Highlands and Islands to the Campbells, MacKenzies and the Gordon Earls of Huntly in their different areas. In the pursuit of royal policy to ensure that clan chiefs took personal responsibility for the actions of their clansmen, the Bishop of the Isles succeeded

in convincing several of the principal leaders to agree to the Statutes
of Iona (1609, developed further in 1616), which required them,
under serious penalty, to attend the Privy Council in Edinburgh
each year to answer for their behaviour. Other regulations included
limitations on the number of men in their following and the
bearing of arms, although an attempt to insist on the destruction
of birlinns was seen to be unreasonable as they were the only form
of peaceful transport in the Isles. As well as directing their heirs
to be educated in English in the Lowlands, the statutes required
chiefs to dismantle their Gaelic learned orders, abandoning the
bardic traditions of their clans. Both of these conditions were seen
as serious threats to Gaelic culture. Their residences were to be
fixed and well-maintained, their lands set to tenants in a systematic
way, and the parish kirk supported. As excessive consumption of
alcohol was considered to be a major factor in the incidence of
violence, there were measures to control the import of wines and
spirits. Even though these statutes were widely flouted, they gave
the crown important tools in dealing with recalcitrant subjects, but
the actual impact of the statutes was not anticipated. The financial
costs of weeks of residence in Edinburgh, attending the Privy
Council, and of educating their children in the Lowlands, not to
mention the dangers of exposure to the more luxurious lifestyles
of their southern equals, were major factors in the financial ruin of
many of the leading chiefs by the eighteenth century.

One component of the Gaelic learned orders that did flourish
until the start of the eighteenth century was the practice of medicine,
particularly by the wider Beaton family, who served leading families
in Islay, Mull and Skye and parts of the mainland. Their approach
continued to be conservative, based on Gaelic translations of
Greek, Arabic and medieval European writings, and founded on
the use of medicinal herbs. Around 1610, Angus Beaton, of the
medical family of Husabost in Skye, was sent for training under
the famous Duncan Connacher, who spent much of his time with
the MacDougalls at Dunollie but was continually travelling round
Argyll to treat patients. Beaton's training consisted of observing
Connacher at work but he was also set the task of copying out by
hand useful extracts of books ranging from Hippocrates and Galen
to treatises from the medical schools of Montpellier and Salerno.
From his habit of adding marginal notes we know that he and

1. Lismore Geology: a. limestone strata distorted by heat and pressure; b. resistant dyke of intruded rock above Loch Fiart, with Creag Island and Cruachan in the distance; c. granite erratic boulder above Point; d. natural arch and raised beach near Port Ramsay.

2. Traces of rig-and-furrow cultivation at Portcharron.

3. Port Ramsay from the top of Glas Dhruim, Alisrath, with the line of white croft houses to the right.

4. The broken stone at Cloichlea. The cup marks are on the nearest face of the largest stone.

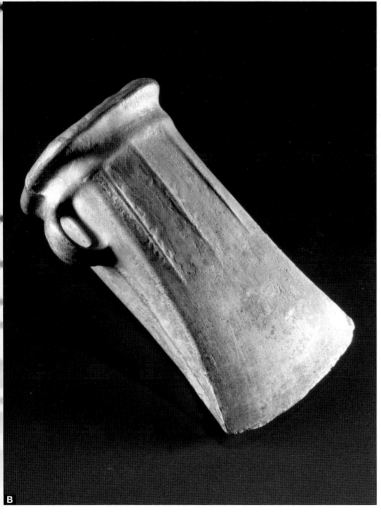

5a. Neolithic axe head (130mm × 80mm); b. Bronze Age socketed axe (length 80mm) found on Barr Mòr (reproduced with the permission of the National Museum of Scotland).

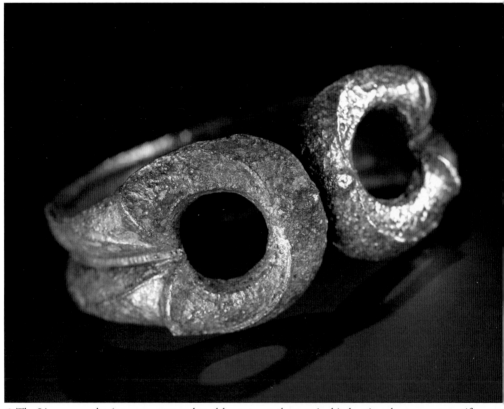

6. The Lismore armlet (97mm × 93mm; breadth 42mm at the terminals) showing the trumpet motifs on the terminals (reproduced with the permission of the National Museum of Scotland).

7a. Cnoc Aingeal, a Bronze Age cairn near Bachuil House; b. Dun Chrubain, an Iron Age fortified dwelling at Dalnarrow on the south-east coast of Lismore.

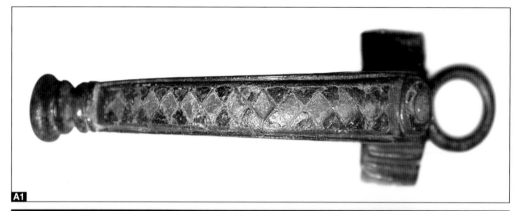

8a. Archaeological finds from Lismore: 1. Enamelled Roman brooch (length approx. 6cm) from the foundation layer at Tirfuir Broch; 2. Medieval pennanular clothes fastener (diameter 4cm) from Achinduin; 3. Medieval Jew's harp from Achinduin (reproduced with the permission of the Lismore Museum). b. Celtic church bell (height 82 mm) from Kilmichael Glassary, later protected by an elaborated medieval shrine, not illustrated (reproduced with the permission of the National Museum of Scotland).

A3

B

9. Niall Livingstone, Baron of Bachuil, holding St Moluag's staff.

10. Display in the Lismore Museum showing (lower) fragments of an eighth-century gravestone and (upper) part of a fourteenth- or fifteenth-century Iona School gravestone, with a rare 'tau-headed stave'.

11a. Achinduin Castle; b. Coeffin Castle, showing beach clearance for hauling up boats, and (right) part of a tidal fish trap.

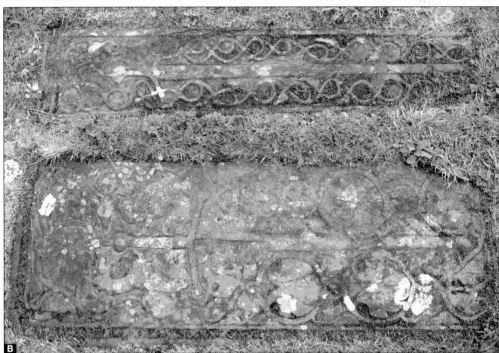

12 Gravestones in Lismore kirkyard: a. a fourteenth- or fifteenth-century Iona School stone showing a Viking-style sword and botanical details; above the sword hilt a stylised goose looks down at a hound chasing a stag; b. a sixteenth-century tomb chest lid commemorating Donald Stewart of Invernahyle; the style of swords, plant scrolls and mythical creatures (lion and birdlike unicorn) is similar to those on stones at Kilmichael Glassary. The accompanying stone (above), attributed to Stewart's Carmichael armour bearer is probably of an earlier period.

13. An early (c.1860) photographic portrait of a Lismore islander, identified as Hugh Cameron, in his younger days as a sailor. Aged 45, he gave evidence as a crofter in Killean to the Napier Commissioners in 1883 (from the Lismore Museum Photographic Archive).

14 Lismore Industry: a. Donald McIntyre's sawpit outside the boat-building cave at Sailean; b. the lime-burning complex at Sailean, showing the two more recent kilns, the coal store (right) and the quarry behind.

15 Sailing smacks at Sailean Pier in the nineteenth century. Note the two clinker-built dinghies, front left, which are typical of the boats built on Lismore. From the Erskine Beveridge Collection (Courtesy of RCAHMS). Copied from *Wanderings With a Camera 1888–1898.*)

16 Dr Alexander Carmichael and Mrs Carmichael at the Cross of Clanamachrie, Taynuilt (reproduced with the permission of the National Museums Scotland).

Connacher were on Lismore in December 1611 and sometime in 1612, and at Achnacroish in July 1613, in between long spells at Dunollie, shorter visits to Muckairn, Ardchonell, Castle Stalker and Glen Creran, and a return to Skye. It seems that there were patients on the island who justified visits from the most important doctor in the area.

The Triumph of the Campbells

Lismore may have been at the limit of the Campbell empire in 1470 but, with a chilling single-mindedness, and assisted by royal patronage, successive earls and chiefs of cadet branches extended their power over the west from Kintyre to Ardnamurchan, filling the void left by the Lords of the Isles. Following an already well-established pattern of behaviour, the Campbells were more likely to use their lawyers than their warriors in securing more land.

The first major development arose out of the troubled relationship between the Glenorchy Campbells and the MacGregors of Glenstrae. The Lords of Glenorchy had been more than willing to make use of fighting bands of their neighbours to guard their boundaries, for example as keepers of Kilchuirn Castle, and to impose their will on landowners round Loch Tay. However, by the mid-sixteenth century the threat that the MacGregors posed to the Lowland fringe was becoming a matter of national concern. They had become a serious embarrassment to the Campbells, who were increasingly involved as agents of the crown. The rapid expansion of the Glenorchy estates had outstripped their ability to protect themselves from raiding so that, when Grey Colin deprived the MacGregors of their traditional lands in Glenstrae, he had to look for support to the Camerons and the Argyll Campbells in resisting the furious onslaught of the MacGregors. With this assistance he survived the perils of the 1560s, and appeared to have brought the matter to a conclusion with the public beheading of their chief, Gregor MacGregor, in 1570, but the increasingly reckless MacGregors continued to cause trouble. The crisis came in 1603 when a raiding band ambushed and destroyed a party of Colquhouns in Glen Fruin. Archibald the Grim, 7th Earl of Argyll, accepted a royal commission to deal with the MacGregors on condition that he would be awarded the

MacDonald lands in Kintyre; by 1607 these had passed in due course into Campbell hands. The MacDonalds of Dunivaig, ruined by their continuing feud with the Macleans of Duart and in trouble with the government, were in no position to oppose this transfer. Indeed they were shortly to lose their heartland on Islay. Heavily in debt, Dunivaig sold out to Campbell of Cawdor in 1611 and, from that time, the power base of 'Clan Donald South' lay in the MacDonnell lands in Antrim in Northern Ireland.

The next opportunity arose in Ardnamurchan. Archibald, 4th Earl of Argyll, had acquired the feudal superiority of the lands of the MacIains (septs of the MacDonalds) in the mid-sixteenth century, on the marriage of the heiress of Ardnamurchan into the Robertson clan. By 1605 the MacIains realised that they had no documentary evidence supporting their right to occupy the lands, and in due course Argyll intervened to install a tacksman on Ardnamurchan and a keeper of the castle of Mingary. In the resulting rebellion of the MacIains, they were hunted down and effectively exterminated with the blessing of the government. By 1625 the Campbells were occupiers as well as the feudal superiors of much of the peninsula.

They were soon to experience the full force of MacDonald revenge. In a time of extreme political complexity, the rise of the Covenanter movement in Scotland and the outbreak of the English Civil War brought Catholic Irish mercenaries, including MacDonnells from Antrim, into Scotland in support of Charles I. These men were battle-hardened from continental wars, and they were led by Alastair MacColla, whose father and brothers had been driven out of MacDonald lands on Colonsay and imprisoned by the Campbells. His religious convictions ensured that Archibald Campbell, now Marquess of Argyll, was on the side of the Covenanters, rather than supporting the king, the traditional Campbell position. MacColla and his men were the key factors in a series of victories over the Covenanting forces credited to Montrose (Tippermuir, Inverlochy and Auldearn), but their main preoccupation was the destruction of Campbell power in Scotland and the recovery of Kintyre by Clan Donald.

Having devastated Inveraray and much of Argyll in the autumn of 1644 on the way to defeating a mainly Campbell force at Inverlochy on February 1645, MacColla broke away from

Montrose in September, after the Battle of Kilsyth, to resume the work. His forces worked their way systematically through the lands of the Argyll and Glenorchy Campbells, killing as many as 2,000 and destroying any property they could not carry off. Glenorchy archives record that their entire property 'between the Ford of the Lyon and the Point of Lismore' was burnt, with losses assessed at £800,000 Scots. Many of the leading families suffered serious loss of life, although Patrick Campbell managed to hold Barcaldine Castle. However, in the face of all of this devastation, Lismore itself was spared because of its connections with the royalist Stewarts of Appin.

These were violent times but it is clear from contemporary accounts that the single-minded ruthlessness and cruelty of the MacColla campaign in Argyll was seen as exceptional. The extent of the slaughter of MacDonalds in the infamous Massacre of Glencoe was very modest compared with what happened to the Campbells in the 1640s. At times the Campbell response was also brutal. The MacDougalls, who had for 200 years acted for the Earls of Argyll in Lorn and Lismore, made the tactical error of siding with the invading royalists. When MacColla was driven out of Scotland in 1647 the MacDougall garrison of Dunaverty, possibly representing a quarter to a third of the fighting strength of the clan, was put to the sword. Their property on Kerrera was destroyed and Dunollie Castle besieged. The Lamonts, further south in Cowal, suffered a similar fate and the full force of Campbell vengeance was focused on the Macleans of Duart, who are said to have brought 1,000 men to support Montrose and MacColla at the Battle of Kilsyth.

These years showed the extraordinary energy and organisation of the Campbells. The Argyll and Glenorchy lands were brought back to productivity and, by 1650, Lowlanders were being 'planted' as tenants in Kintyre, where they were expected to introduce more advanced husbandry as well as to be generally more reliable than the MacDonalds they replaced. However, it was the erratic behaviour of the marquess that posed the main threat to the future of the Campbell empire. As the leading figure in the Covenanting party, he took part, in 1650, in the defeat by Cromwell at Dunbar, and in the crowning of the future Charles II as King of Scots, but when Charles decided not to marry his daughter Argyll withdrew and took no part in the campaign that ended at the Battle of Worcester. Possibly his most serious error was to cooperate with Cromwell in the suppression of the royalist rebellion under the Earl of Glencairn in 1655. Following the Restoration of the Stewart monarchy in 1660, Argyll was judged to have been guilty of treason and was beheaded by The Maiden in Edinburgh in 1661.

His son, Lord Lorn, who had a respectable royalist record, was pardoned by the king and the earldom was restored in 1663 by a government that recognised that a power vacuum had developed in the west. Having retained all of the lands acquired by his predecessors, Archibald, 9th Earl of Argyll, began now to move against the Macleans of Duart who, ironically, had been faithful to the Stuarts during the decades of conflict and occupation, sustaining heavy losses (700 of the Maclean name alone) and the death of their chief at the Battle of Inverkeithing (1651) against Cromwell. Argyll's father had bought up Duart's debts, estimated at £120,000 by 1657, and in 1673 the earl obtained a 'decreet of removal' against the Macleans. The legal right to their lands in Mull, Tiree and Morvern was one thing but the actual possession took another six years at least and involved armed expeditions to Mull and dealing with an invasion of Argyll. Difficulties with rebellious Macleans continued and it was not until the 1690s that they were able to make full use of these new areas.

Meanwhile, the Lords of Glenorchy were following the clan pattern, acquiring the mounting debts of the Earls of Caithness and succeeding to the title by 1677 in spite of local opposition. Although the king intervened in favour of the Sinclair heir, the Glenorchy Campbells were compensated with the title of Earl of Breadalbane, achieving the same rank as the Argylls.

Thus, by the end of the seventeenth century, Lismore was surrounded by Campbell lands, although the future was uncertain. The security of the Argyll empire had been threatened by the execution of the 8th Earl, and his son was also in trouble by 1681. Having stretched himself financially, and being surrounded by enemies who resented Campbell domination and the harsh treatment of the Macleans, he was manoeuvred into a position where he was unable to sign the Test Act, affirming his allegiance to Protestantism. Tried for treason and sentenced to death, Archibald Campbell fled to the Netherlands from where he led the disastrous

Scottish campaign of the Monmouth rebellion against James VII in 1685. He followed his father to an assignation with The Maiden and the Campbell lands were ravaged yet again, with the Macleans taking the opportunity for revenge. It looked like the end for the Campbells but they were very soon to move to an unassailable position with the arrival of William and Mary.

The Glorious Revolution and the Jacobite Response

Three years after the execution of his father, the 10th Earl of Argyll made his way to the Netherlands to join William of Orange, taking part in the invasion of England and the Glorious Revolution of 1688. From that time political decisions became much simpler for the Campbells. In spite of their uneasy relationships with the House of Stuart in the past, many of the western clans, including the Macleans, MacNeils, Stewarts of Appin, MacIains of Glencoe, and Clanranald became firm adherents of James VII, who, during his short reign, had proved sympathetic to their needs. Not all Jacobites embraced Catholicism: many adhered to the Episcopal Church, but they were united against the Campbells, who were firmly in the Presbyterian camp and able to return to their traditional role of serving the reigning monarch.

The Jacobites quickly rose in rebellion and, led by the charismatic John Graham of Claverhouse, inflicted a major defeat on the government army under General Hugh Mackay at Killiecrankie. The death of Graham, and determined resistance when they tried to march south to the Lowlands through Dunkeld, caused the Jacobite forces to disperse and the final defeat came at Cromdale in 1690. Argyll, building up his credibility with the new king, raised the first of several Campbell Regiments of Foot for the new British Army and took part in a campaign to pacify the Isles, taking the opportunity to look after his interests in Mull. With confidence fully restored, the earl was created 1st Duke of Argyll in 1701, and successive dukes would dominate the West Highlands and Islands, not to mention Scottish politics after the Union, for more than two centuries.

In spite of taking no part in the Glorious Revolution, Breadalbane had gained the confidence of the new regime and was employed and generously financed as an intermediary with the Jacobite clans, calling a memorable meeting of clan chiefs in June 1691 at the ruined castle of Achallader. For those who had failed to submit to the new government, including the MacIains of Glencoe (whose MacDonald clansmen were, incidentally, responsible for regular raids into Breadalbane's lands), a target date of 1 January 1692 was set for signing the Oath of Allegiance. The response of the aged MacIain was slow: he was detained at Barcaldine Castle, and he chose to submit on the last day of December to the military rather than the civil authorities at Fort William. This gave the opportunity for the government to use MacIain as an example, and a company of government troops under Campbell of Glenlyon duly carried out the treacherous Massacre of Glencoe. Breadalbane was widely held to be responsible but his own response at the time, and the judgement of history, indicate that the Campbell forces and Glenlyon, a Breadalbane cadet, were tools in the hands of the Master of Stair, the Secretary of State for Scotland. When the Jacobites next rose in 1715, Argyll was the commander of the government forces, frustrating the ambitions of the ineffectual Earl of Mar. Once again, the position of the Breadalbane Campbells was difficult to pin down, with some clansmen, led by the earl's eldest son, joining the abortive invasion of Argyll and taking part in the inconclusive Battle of Sheriffmuir. The earl averted trouble by disinheriting him in favour of his younger brother and, thereafter, the Breadalbanes were pillars of the Union and the government.

How Lismore was Owned

On 17 April 1460, James III granted the hereditary lordship of Lorn, including Lismore, to Colin Campbell, 1st Earl of Argyll. In return, the new Lord of Lorn and his successors were obliged to ensure the rule of law within their marches; to provide hospitality to the king, his officials and followers as required; and to supply fully trained manpower, weapons and transport (including galleys) in time of war or serious unrest. Even for Lismore these resources were substantial. The 1692 muster of 'fencible men between sixteen and sixty' on the island included 96 names, 55 swords and 41 guns.

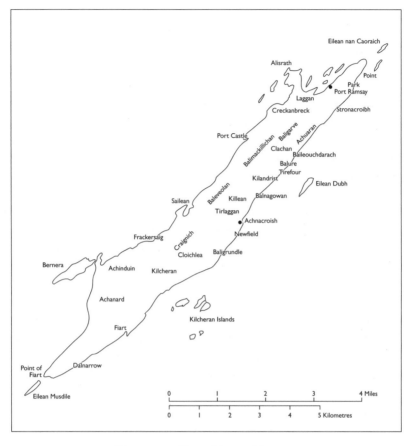

Figure 7.1   Townships on Lismore.

If these feudal obligations were met, the lordship would be effectively freehold, without rent, unless the male line failed or the heir was a minor, in which case the lordship would revert, at least temporarily, to the crown. Of course, although it was not normally in his best interest, the king could deprive a feu holder of his land at will and it was not uncommon for a new king to take the opportunity to redistribute land and titles to his supporters. At this time the feudal system was evolving towards the development of fully documented land-ownership in the wake of the collapse, at the Reformation, of a legal system dominated by the Church (Chapter 8). This evolution culminated in the establishment of the

Register of Sasines in 1617, and it became increasingly important to have written parchment charters to ensure security of tenure. With the agreement of the crown, feudal tenure could be exchanged for money, as in the sale of part of Lismore by Stewart of Appin to Argyll in 1508.

Colin Campbell's possession of Lorn and Lismore was far from straightforward and, in achieving the lordship, his gains were more political than economic. As the Lords of Glenorchy had a legal claim on one-third of the lands of the lordship, through the marriage of Janet Stewart to Colin Campbell of Glenorchy, the latter became, in turn, the feudal vassal of Argyll with similar rights and obligations. His successors continued as landowners on Lismore and elsewhere in Lorn for nearly three centuries but their position as vassals of Argyll, even for their original lands in Glenorchy, was a continual irritant. In the same way, from 1490 the Stewarts held land in Appin and the north of Lismore, and the MacDougalls had Dunollie and Kerrera, both as vassals of Argyll. The relationship with the MacDougalls was more complex, incorporating their long-standing hereditary rights to acts as baillies for Lorn and to foster the heir to the lordship. Argyll's income from Lismore was also reduced by the diversion of the rents of the south-west quarter of the island to support the cathedral (Chapter 6). The pattern of land ownership becomes more difficult to understand in the later seventeenth century when Argyll and Glenorchy began to grant feus of individual townships to cadets of the clan who were also non-resident.

Although there seems to have been some fluctuation in the ownership of parts of the island over these years (1460–1734), the Glenorchy holding was mainly a diagonal band across Lismore, including the townships of Baligrundle (with Tierewin), Achnacroish, Tirlaggan, Killean, Balliveolan and Balimakillichan (including Castle Chaben or Coeffin) as well the unidentified Pennyfurt. North of the Glenorchy holding, the lands of Killandrist, Portcharron and Kinlochan (later called Taynlochan, next to Clachan) had been acquired by Argyll by 1508, but Stewart of Appin appears to have held on to the remainder of the north end at least until the 1640s, when he was able to protect Lismore against the depredations of MacColla. Argyll owned Balnagowan, until it was feued to Campbell of Ardnamurchan in 1651, and much of the rest of the island, although the church lands in the south-west had a complicated history after the Reformation (Chapter 8).

When the Campbells arrived as landlords the island had, for centuries, been divided up into townships (the natural units of land area, with associated settlements), rated according to a notional rental value in merks (two-thirds of a pound Scots). The names of at least two townships (Pennyfurt and Pennybacuil), and early church grants (Chapter 6), indicate the existence of an alternative valuation system: the pennyland, equivalent to around 10 acres. The landlords let out their land, normally by township, or by part of a township, to individual tacksmen in return for payment of rent, originally in kind (grain, cattle, poultry and other products such as butter and cheese) and generated by the work of the many small tenants and cottars on each holding who had no formal rights. On Glenorchy's land on Lismore, the six merkland of Baligrundle was a centre for whisky production, and this is reflected in the tack (lease) of 1706, which required the new tacksman, John Campbell, to provide two quarts of aquavitae each year. Balliveolan was a three merkland (half was let to Archibald MacGilleune as a '20 shilling land' in 1629, see below), Balimakillichan was assessed at four merks, and Killean and Cloichlea were each two merklands.

By the seventeenth century, some Lismore tacks were recorded in written form (relatively few Glenorchy tacks have survived) and by the middle of the century the rents were mainly in cash. The tacksman was also responsible for delivering the teind and the 'viccarage' (direct support to the parish clergy) in money, and, in some cases, the estate also required rent in advance in the form of a gerssom (grassum), as a form of security. For example, the 1675 rental shows that, in addition to rents of £230 and £160 Scots, tacksmen in Ballimakillichan and Balliveolan were required to deliver a further £100 per year for each of five years. The duration of tacks, generally less than 10 years in line with Lowland practice, did not necessarily mean that tenure was insecure as trusted tacksmen would expect the regular renewal of tacks, but it did provide the landowner with tools for change. On the other hand, there was a risk of encouraging short-term exploitative farming. In more remote and less fertile areas the Campbells were prepared to grant tacks for life, and, where appropriate, they offered 'steelbow' tenure, providing seed, implements and livestock to set up a tenant but exacting a higher proportion of the resulting produce in rent.

The role of the tacksmen was not simply to manage the farming of the land. They were links in the feudal chain, acting as the lord's agents, and providing various 'services' as required. For example, in 1629 half of Balliveolan was set to Archibald MacGilleune on condition that, in addition to rent, he would be responsible for 'hosting' (raising and leading the fighting men, 'the host', on his land), 'hunting' (supporting his lord when hunting in the neighbourhood), 'stenting' (collection of tiends and other financial liabilities), and 'ariage and carriage' (transport of rent in kind, carriage of people, and providing messengers as required). The military nature of the feudal system persisted well into the seventeenth century. For example, the service required by Argyll for Cloichlea in 1651 amounted to half a galley and the manning of six of its oars. On top of these many burdens, if the tacksman died during the course of his tack, the landlord exacted a 'calp' from the estate (normally the best horse) to pay for the funeral. Although this tradition was outlawed in 1617 by the Scottish Parliament for being unduly oppressive, it continued in Glenorchy's estates until the end of the seventeenth century. In the sequence of feudal responsibilities, the cottars would be expected to provide the tacksman with labour at sowing and harvest, and in cutting and carrying peat fuel.

Because these rights and responsibilities set the tacksman apart from the people, it was not uncommon for the landlord to introduce a trusted individual from outside the island. For example, the tack of 1629 includes a clause that Archibald MacGilleune, presumably a stranger, should be resident in Balliveolan, but Killean was set to a Stewart of Appin who was apparently not resident. However, the 'middle class' aspect of tacksmen in this period should not be over-emphasised as there is no evidence on the island of any form of higher-class housing. Where resident, the tacksman appears to have enjoyed a similar lifestyle to that of his tenants and cottars. The only exception to these arrangements was the small estate of Bachuil, held effectively in freehold by the Macleays in return for their traditional duties as dewars, guarding St Moluag's staff on behalf of the Lord of Lorn. Any tradition of the tacksman as 'first amongst equals' on Lismore finally disappeared in the seventeenth century with the feuing or wadsetting (mortgaging) of townships to non-resident Campbell cadets (Chapter 9).

Life in the Lismore Townships

Some idea of the pattern of life on Lismore from the sixteenth to the eighteenth century can be gained from the rentals, registers of tacks, factors' or chamberlains' accounts, and court records in the Breadalbane archive. During much of the period, Lismore court business, covering both estate matters and the exercise of law, seems to have been done on the mainland, at the same time as other Glenorchy business, for example at Drishaig (near Kilchurn Castle) and Ferlochan (near Barcaldine Castle). In the early decades of the eighteenth century the Campbells of Barcaldine acted as the baillies of Benderloch and Lismore on behalf of Glenorchy, but, after they took possession of land on the island, and until the withdrawal of hereditary jurisdictions in 1747, they held their own court at Taynlochan (near Clachan).

As elsewhere in Scotland, the arable land would have been divided into infield (the more fertile areas, receiving most of the available manure and cropped each year) and outfield (less fertile, left uncultivated for several years in succession and then cropped for one or two years), although it is likely than the proportion of outfield on Lismore was small. The traditional crop was the six-row bere barley but, by the end of the eighteenth century, oats had come to predominate and bere growing continued mainly to support whisky production. An important feature of Lismore farming was the early inclusion of improved grass ley within the head dyke.

The arable land was drained by ploughing the soil up into long rigs, which seem to have been narrower (probably less than 2m) than was common in the Lowlands, with intervening furrows to carry water away. As permanent features of the infield, they can still be traced in many parts of the island (Plate 2; see also Plate 1b), in some cases associated with great piles of stones cleared from the land. A great deal of effort was required each year to rebuild the rigs, and to transport and spread manure and seaweed in preparation for sowing cereals. Some of the labour was provided by horses, rather than oxen as in the Lowlands, but, due to the rockiness of the land, there must have been a great deal of spade work. Cereal harvesting was by sickle, with followers binding and stooking sheaves, and later gleaning any lost grain. Where a holding was cultivated jointly by several tenants, each had a defined area of rig and furrow, at least for the current growing season. The distribution of these areas across the holding, allowing each tenant to have his fair share of the better land, resulted in the intermingled pattern of division called runrig.

Although cereal growing was more dominant than in other parts of Argyll, cattle rearing and small-scale dairy production were important components of the economy of each holding. Livestock exploited the areas of rough grazing that could not be ploughed, consumed crop wastes producing manure for the next crop, provided important supplements to a diet dominated by grain and generated income from sale of young stock and dairy products. Surviving testaments show that cattle, sheep and horses represented a major part of the wealth of seventeenth-century tacksmen. The challenge was to keep the cows out of the corn and the seasonal pattern of life was dominated by estate regulations to keep livestock outside well-maintained head dykes of earth and stone until harvest. Specifically for Lismore, the date of removal was 15 May, rather than 1 May, to let the livestock benefit from spring growth of the grass leys within the head dyke. The landlord's ground officer played an important part in enforcing these regulations, operating a 'poindfauld' where straying cattle were enclosed; they were liberated only after 'proclaiming at the kirk' and the payment of a fine.

Tenants were ordered to remove their animals further away to sheilings from 8 June to 15 July. This was possible in some parts of the island, particularly in the south near the rocky ridge of Barr Mòr, but the absence of suitable areas in the north forced some tenants to move them to the small outlying islands. This seems to have had the added benefit of providing an opportunity to supplement their diet by fishing. Under the estate regulations for Lismore, only one or two horses 'for carriage purposes', cows that were too weak to make it to the sheiling, and a milk cow needed to feed an invalid, were permitted inside the head dyke during the cereal-growing season.

In an attempt to vary the diet of the population and to comply with acts of the Scottish Parliament that were intended to encourage agricultural Improvement, in the first half of the seventeenth century the Glenorchy baron courts set regulations to require tacksmen to grow small areas of wheat and pease, and to establish kailyards where greens could be grown and seedling trees protected until they could be planted out on the holding. The records of the Lismore court include numerous prosecutions for non-compliance between 1615 and 1642; eventually, as in other parts of Scotland, the unsuitability of the land for wheat, in particular, was recognised and the regulations were largely ignored by the end of the century. The lack of success in encouraging kailyards confirms the impression that, throughout the West Highlands and Islands, vegetables were not regarded as sustaining food.

Bere and oats, in the form of porridge and bannocks, and in soup, were the dietary staples right up into modern times. The potato did not make an impact until well into the eighteenth century. Originally, the grain was threshed by hand in small quantities as required and ground to meal using simple stone querns. In setting up water-powered mills to mechanise milling, feudal landlords invested capital in expectation of long-term income from the rent of the mill. The miller, in turn, exacted his proportion of the meal from the tenants, who were obliged to use the mill. Glenorchy rentals indicate that tacksmen were also expected to pay a cash multer (multure) to the landlord with their rent. It has been claimed that the scarcity of surviving querns is a consequence of their destruction by landlords determined to ensure that all the estate grain went through the mill.

The principal mill on the Glenorchy lands on Lismore was established at Achnacroish in the early seventeenth century, and the island court records continuing conflict between the miller, who was accused of not maintaining the mill, and the tenants, who refused to use the mill and to do their share of the maintenance work. Some resolution was achieved in 1641 when the court set the multure due to the miller at a peck for every three bolls ground (around 2 per cent), and made it clear that the tenants were responsible for upkeep and repairs, but the relationship was always an uneasy one, with the miller seen as parasitic on tacksman and tenant. In later years there were also chronic problems with the estate mill at Baligrundle/Kilcheran. In 1728 Alexander Campbell of Clenamachrie, tacksman of Baligrundle, and John MacIlchonnell, his tenant, were granted 'lawburrows' (formal legal protection) against 'Alexander Campbell of Airds, John MacVicar in Barvrack, Donald Campbell of Airds, Hugh Stewart in Clochlea and 22 others from Lismore' who were accused of 'conceiving a deadly hatred against [them], casting down and demolishing the mill and its watergang [lade]'. This conflict arose because the Campbells of Airds were proprietors of Cloichlea, bordering on Kilcheran Loch, which fed the mill lade.

On Argyll's land, there were meal mills, powered by outflows of the two other freshwater lochs at Balnagowan and Miller's Port (below Fiart Loch), and there must have been a further mill at some time at the north end of the island on the Allt a' Mhuillin (Mill Burn) near the modern farm of Laggan. It is not known where the grain from the church lands was milled.

The responsibility for building homes, byres and barns on the townships fell to the tenant, although the landlord became the legal owner, and could charge his tacksmen and tenants for damage and depreciation. As timber was scarce, the tenant would have rights to his roof timbers if he was required to leave. Under these conditions, the standard was basic: dry-stone walling without windows; low wall heights with the roof supported on wooden crucks reaching nearly to the ground; thatching, probably with reeds from the freshwater lochs; and a central hearth with smoke escaping through the thatch. Fuel for cooking and heating was in short supply. Aware that the peat resources in parts of the island were running out, the Glenorchy landlords tried to enforce the use of the Lowland peat spade, which reduced waste by cutting horizontally, rather than the traditional tuskar, and the Lismore court records for the 1620s include several prosecutions for non-compliance.

On his visit to the island in 1771 Rev. John Walker reported that there was no wood or peat on the island and that the inhabitants burned unsatisfactory 'doughy peat' (*moine iobach*), moulded from organic-rich loch deposits, to the detriment of their complexions. This was something of an exaggeration as peat was still being cast from small peat banks around Tirfuir, Stronacroibh, Tirlaggan and other parts of the island. For example, in 1824 Colin Campbell of Baleveolan wrote to Campbell of Barcaldine asking for access by his tenants to the Balure moss. Peat was also not the only source of fuel as, in 1686, the Campbells had reached a formal agreement with the Macleans of Kingairloch for each family on Lismore to collect timber to the extent of six loads of a six-oared boat each year from their forest across Loch Linnhe. Even though hazel and rowan were spared, this led to the extinction of the Kingairloch woods within a century and, thereafter, many of the islanders were forced to devote considerable time and effort to cutting and carrying peat from Morvern and Benderloch.

The control exerted over the people of the island was not restricted to farming, milling and housing but extended over the whole economy. The island court fixed prices for craft products such as woven cloth and even appointed cunstars (tasters) to check on the quality and value of ale brewed on the island. Across their extensive estates the Glenorchy lairds laid down very comprehensive regulations for the improvement of agriculture and for everyday life. For example, in addition to the measures already described for cropping, livestock husbandry and milling, the 1621 and 1623 Acts of the Laird of Glenorchy dealt with muirburn in spring (six 'honest neighbours' to be present when near trees); control of poaching; maintenance of the standard of tenants' buildings; tree planting; pig keeping (prohibited); protection against wolves; control of crows, rooks and magpies; compensation for losses caused by unauthorised grazing; conflict resolution between neighbours; payments for legal representation; maintenance of smiddies; penalties for housing strangers, stealing sacks and damaging trees; fining of wives drinking alone in a 'broustar house'; protection of river banks; harvesting bracken; control of scab in horses (isolated or thrown over a cliff); and arrangements for intestate deaths (half to the laird and half to the poor). Certainly, in terms of the agricultural measures, the Glenorchy Campbells were well ahead of most Lowland landlords of the time.

Life in the Campbell Empire

Unlike other clan groupings, the Campbells succeeded in maintaining and expanding their empire over several hundred years of turbulent history. This was partly the result of a relatively unbroken line of able, ambitious and single-minded leaders, not only of the senior Argyll branch, but also of the Glenorchy Campbells and other cadets. For much of the period the members of the wider clan appreciated what could be gained by solidarity, and coherence was achieved by regular Campbell councils. When things did go badly wrong (for example, the bid for domination by Glenorchy and Ardkinglass which resulted in the murder of Campbell of Cawdor in 1592, and the execution of two successive earls in 1661 and 1685) the structure held firm, and the crown found it inadvisable to interfere with such a powerful force for order in the west. When the succession appeared to be in doubt there was early identification of the heir (e.g. the childless 5th Earl, although still in his 30s, formally recognised his brother), and there was more than one occasion when the future of the clan and its cadets was ensured by fathers and sons taking different sides.

Ambition cannot be fulfilled without resources. The Argyll Campbells founded their economy on the relative fertility of their lands round Loch Awe and in Cowal; but it was their service to the crown, in roles ranging from local justiciar (magistrate) to chancellor of Scotland, that brought in the money to fund expansion and to survive severe setbacks such as the devastations by MacColla and the Macleans in the seventeenth century. This continuity of income from the state purse and their early recognition of the commercial, as well as the military, value of land, gave them the edge over clans such as the MacDonalds. As a result, by the eighteenth century, they were able to raise a host of 5,000 fighting men and Glenorchy could contribute at least 1,000 more. These forces were on a scale similar to those commanded by the crown, but the Campbells also dominated the west coast by investing heavily in naval power and by securing the necessary resources such as commercial oakwoods and skilled labour. For example, a rare surviving account for the construction and fitting out of a 16-oared birlinn for the Campbells of Glenorchy by their hereditary shipwrights, the Clann Mhic Gille Chonaill, shows that in 1635 it cost £257 8s 4d (Scots). Dr Donald McWhannell has estimated that this was equivalent to one-third of the annual income from their lands in Argyll. Although such a boat could have a useful life of 30 years, the cost of maintaining fleets of galleys for peaceful and warlike activities would have been very considerable. But the mobility achieved was impressive: for example, for the marriage ceremonies uniting the Campbells with the powerful families of O'Neill and O'Donnell in 1569, 32 galleys carried 4,000 men from Islay to Ulster. Nevertheless, in spite of commanding such military and naval power, the Campbells were more likely to use the courts, exploiting their experience in the law as justiciars in the king's service to achieve their aims.

For the people of Lismore, membership of this expanding empire had several consequences: very tight social control, imposition of Lowland values (short leases, high rents, commercial valuation of land), very early introduction of agricultural Improvement, and tight regulation of prices and wages. All of these constraints on a Gaelic-speaking community were implemented through a baron court, normally held off the island, whose language was Scots. Baron courts elsewhere in Scotland dealt with a range of minor and major criminal cases, but the very brief records of the Glenorchy court are dominated by estate issues (sowing wheat and pease, casting peats, damaging roads, cutting timber, etc.), with little opportunity given for the resolution of conflict and punishment for crime on the island. On the other hand, ownership by the Campbells provided a high degree of protection, for example from the chronic raiding during the *Linn nan Creach* which undermined the lives and livelihoods of those on other islands. Ironically, when Campbell protection failed in the 1640s, it was the intervention of the Stewarts of Appin that saved Lismore from MacColla. Since no major landowner actually lived on the island, much of the regulation of life and work must have been done by the minister, by resident tacksmen, and by estate officials such as ground officers. It is likely that these circumstances, and the relative isolation of the island, led to a coherent and independent-minded community. The court books provide ample evidence of their willingness to defy estate regulations.

Bibliography

The Black Book of Glenorchy (1855). Privately printed by T. Constable, Edinburgh, for the Marquess of Breadalbane.

Bannerman, J. (1998) *The Beatons: A Medical Kindred in the Classical Gaelic Tradition*. Edinburgh: John Donald.

Boardman, S. (2006) *The Campbells, 1250–1513*. Edinburgh: John Donald.

Campbell, A. (2002) *A History of Clan Campbell: 2. From Flodden to the Restoration*. Edinburgh: Polygon.

Dawson, J.E.A. (ed.) (1997) *Clan Campbell Letters*. Edinburgh: Scottish History Society.

Gregory, D. (2008) *The History of the Western Highlands and Isles of Scotland, 1493–1625* (facsimile of the 1881 edition). Edinburgh: John Donald.

McKay, M.M. (ed.) (1980) *The Rev. Dr John Walker's Report on the Hebrides of 1764 and 1771*. Edinburgh: John Donald.

Mactavish, D.C. (1935) *The Commons of Argyll*. Lochgilphead: James Annan.

McWhannell, D.C. (2007) 'Campbell Boatbuilding Accounts, 1600 to 1700'. *History Scotland* 7(1), 14–19; 7(2), 18–21.

Munro, J. and Munro, R.W. (1986) *Acts of the Lords of the Isles, 1336–1493*. Edinburgh: Scottish History Society.

Shaw, F.J. (1980) *The Northern and Western Islands of Scotland*. Edinburgh, John Donald.

8

Argyll and the Reformation

In Argyll the Reformation was rapid and decisive, in contrast to much of the Highlands and Islands, where destruction of the Roman Catholic organisation left a void than would not be filled for more than 100 years. As in most aspects of life, change was driven by the Campbell landlords. Archibald, 4th Earl of Argyll was an early convert to Calvinism through contact with John Knox. He demonstrated his conviction by maintaining an illegal Protestant chaplain in his household and, on his deathbed in 1558, he made his son promise to work towards the establishment of a reformed national Church. This son, the 5th Earl, also Archibald, was a leading member of the group of Protestant Lords who dominated the reforming Scottish Parliament in 1560, and he was instrumental in ensuring that the liturgy of the new Church was accessible to Gaelic speakers. Historians judge that the Reformation would have failed in Scotland without the combined resolution of James Stuart, Earl of Moray, and Archibald Campbell. Marriage to Katherine Ruthven ensured that Colin Campbell of Glenorchy was also firmly in the Protestant camp, but neither family could have predicted that, owing to the varying religious outlooks of their rulers, it would take until 1690 before the Church of Scotland could establish a settled Presbyterian structure.

Seeds of the Reformation

In Scotland, as elsewhere in Europe, the pre-Reformation Church was responsible not only for the spiritual life of the country but also for its schools and universities, its hospitals and the support of the poor and needy. Together, the cathedrals, abbeys and priories were major landowners and employers of labour, and the Church was also the principal source of lawyers trained in civil as well as canon law. As access to a notary was essential for all property transactions, landowners had a particular interest in senior appointments.

By the fifteenth and sixteenth centuries the Church was experiencing a serious decline in standards, which threatened all of these aspects of the national life. Although the sexual activity of the supposedly celibate clergy had been a continuing difficulty, other symptoms of secularisation and materialism were widespread: diversion of funds and land; legal malpractice; luxurious lifestyles; priests participating in trades, business and landowning; poor general education and theological training. Senior positions were dominated by placemen of the ruling class, irrespective of suitability, education or age, who could support their patron's political ambitions in parliament and channel financial and other resources. Most spectacularly, illegitimate sons of James V were in charge of the abbeys of Melrose, Kelso and Holyrood, the priories of Coldingham and Whithorn, and the charterhouse of Perth. His most prominent natural son, James Stuart, who shared leadership of the Protestant Lords of the Congregation with Argyll, was made lay commendator of the priory of St Andrews at the age of six. He became Earl of Moray in 1562.

The record of the diocese of Argyll was no different: the last five bishops based on Lismore were Robert Colquhoun (1475–95), son of Colquhoun of Luss, excommunicated for insubordination; David Hamilton (1497–1523), illegitimate son of Lord Hamilton; Robert Montgomery (1525–38), son of the Earl of Eglinton, appointed at 24; William Cunynghame (1539–53), son of the Earl of Glencairn, appointed at 26 and probably not consecrated as a priest; and James Hamilton (1553–80), illegitimate brother of the Hamilton Duke of Châtelherault, probably not consecrated even though he had been unsuccessfully nominated as Archbishop of Glasgow in 1547. Over these years, appointments to the bishopric were arranged jointly by the dominant family of Hamilton (Earls of Arran) and the Campbells (the mother of the 5th Earl of Argyll was a daughter of the Earl of Arran), and there were lengthy vacant periods of 13 months in 1496, 20 months in 1523, and 5 months in 1538 while they sought suitable candidates, predominantly from south-west Scotland.

In view of their origins and the roles expected of them by their patrons as part of the lordly retinue, it is unlikely that these bishops spent much of their time on Lismore, where the cathedral and, presumably, the lodgings of the clergy were rapidly falling into disrepair. Indeed, on 29 April 1462, a 'Papal Indult' was granted to George Lauder, Bishop of Argyll, permitting him to live outside the diocese, in Glasgow, or elsewhere within two days ride of the diocese, because of continuing armed conflict in the area.

Even after the Reformation had undermined his position, Bishop Hamilton continued to live the high life in Edinburgh, dining with Queen Mary on the night of the murder of her husband, Lord Darnley. The Bishops of Argyll did have the potential benefit, in time of insecurity, of the 300-year-old castle of Achinduin, but its spartan accommodation would have been hardly to the taste of aristocrats raised in the Renaissance palaces of the day. They were more likely to seek safety in the modern castle at Saddell, built by Bishop David Hamilton around 1510. Overall, there is little hard evidence for the presence of bishops on Lismore at all after the visit of Bishop Lauder in 1452.

Secularisation was not restricted to the bishops of Argyll. Enjoying the patronage of the Glenorchy Campbells, James MacGregor (alias James Gregorie) trained as a notary, was appointed vicar of his native Fortingall in 1511, and served as Dean of Lismore from 1514 to his death in 1551. Assisted by his brother Duncan, he compiled the *Book of the Dean of Lismore*, a collection of fifteenth- and sixteenth-century Gaelic poetry and a range of older Ossianic material. There is little about the island in the book. The book is the oldest surviving example of written Scots Gaelic using its distinctive orthography, and it demonstrates that at least some of the chapter of the cathedral were fluent in the language. MacGregor was the son of a priest and his eminence in church and law did not stop him, in turn, from fathering at least two sons, Gregor and Dougall. As Sir James MacGregor (using a courtesy title given to senior priests who were not graduates), he held land from the Glenorchy Campbells in Tayside, presumably in gratitude for the many legal services he provided as notary and witness to bonds, sasines and tacks. At a time when Glenorchy was at war with the MacGregor clan, James' son Gregor signed a 'bond of manrent' to Colin Campbell of Glenorchy, recognising him as his chief, and both sons were formally legitimised in 1557, but this did not prevent Gregor from being murdered in 1565. Dougall survived to become chancellor of Lismore.

The Reform Parliament of 1560

The Reformation in Scotland cannot be disentangled from a very complex set of international relations. By 1534, in pursuit of a divorce from Anne Boleyn, Henry VIII had broken from Rome and assumed headship of the Church in England. By this unlikely path England became notionally Protestant, at least during his lifetime. Meanwhile, although there was a significant pro-English group of nobles in Scotland, the country was dominated by Mary of Guise, who was eventually appointed regent in 1554. The French mother of the infant Queen Mary, Mary was firmly in the Catholic camp, with Cardinal Beaton as chancellor. Henry, whose ambitions to unite the two countries by the marriage of his son Edward to Queen Mary had been thwarted by her mother, embarked on a series of raids into Scotland known later as the 'Rough Wooing'. Over four years from 1543, the Earl of Hertford devastated much of the south of Scotland, inflicting a major defeat of the Scots at Pinkie. Fine carved gravestones in Lismore kirkyard commemorate the lives of Donald Stewart of Invernahyle who led the Stewarts of Appin at Pinkie, and his Carmichael armour-bearer. Known as 'Stewart of the Hammers' from his ability to wield blacksmith's hammers in each hand from the age of 16, he survived the battle and lived on to the end of the century. This 'wooing' came to an end in 1548 when the young queen was sent to France.

Meanwhile, new regulations covering doctrine, discipline and administration of the Church were introduced to Scotland in the wake of the Council of Trent (1545–63). These were, however, too late to halt the advance of Protestantism which, although still a minority movement, was being actively propagated through the east and south-west of Scotland by priests returning from study in Germany and Switzerland. The willingness of the Church to burn these heretics was probably critical. The execution of George

Wishart, a disciple of Calvin, in 1545 led in the following year to the murder of Cardinal Beaton and the occupation of St Andrews Castle by a group of Protestant revolutionaries. They were dislodged by French troops brought into Scotland by Mary of Guise, but, surprisingly, not summarily executed. Amongst others, John Knox was sent to serve in French galleys, later being freed to continue his studies in Geneva.

Over the next 12 years the Protestant cause continued to grow in strength, culminating in 1557 in the signing of a bond between members of the aristocracy (the Lords of the Congregation), led by the 4th Earl of Argyll and his son, to establish a reformed Church. This group was particularly coherent because it was bound together by intermarriage as well as faith. Archibald, 5th Earl of Argyll, son of a Hamilton mother, was married to yet another illegitimate child of James V, Jane Stuart, thereby becoming the brother-in-law of the Protestant James Stuart (and also of Mary Queen of Scots). Two international developments in 1558 precipitated direct action: the accession of Elizabeth, Queen of England, who was a firm supporter of Protestantism, reversing the policies of her sister; and the marriage of Queen Mary to the French Dauphin, which effectively brought Scotland under the rule of Catholic France. Scotland became a battlefield between its ancient enemy (England, now, uncomfortably, the Protestant ally of the majority of the nobles) and its ancient ally (France).

In obedience to his promise to his father, Archibald Campbell played a central role in the events of the next two years, taking up a clear Protestant and pro-English position. In response to the lack of action by parliament and by the regent, Mary of Guise, rioting broke out in towns on the east coast, with Lord Ruthven (Glenorchy's father-in-law) leading the iconoclasm in Perth in May 1559, destroying all of the 'idolatrous' art and decoration in the city churches. For over a year Scotland was plunged into a complicated civil war involving not only the religious factions within the country, but also French troops under the command of the regent, and an invading English army invited north by Argyll and the Lords of the Congregation to secure Protestantism. With the death of the regent in June 1560 and an English force surrounding Edinburgh, the way was clear for a reforming parliament to be called.

Meanwhile, Argyll had been active in the West Highlands, presiding in Lorn in August 1559 over an expanded Campbell council, including the major clans of the west, to secure the support of Gaeldom for the Lords of the Congregation. At the meeting was the principal agent for change, John Carswell, a priest devoted to the Protestant cause, who had been brought into the 4th Earl's household around 1549 as notary, chaplain and tutor to his children. He was bound even more closely to the family by his marriage to Margaret, daughter of Campbell of Ardkinglas, Archibald's foster father, and a surviving letter to Katherine Ruthven shows that he was on intimate terms with the Glenorchy Campbells. In preparation for Carswell's role in driving through the Reformation in Argyll, the 5th Earl secured his independence by endowing him with land where he built Carnasserie Castle, a Renaissance tower north of Kilmartin. At the same time, Archibald would have ensured that his bishop, James Hamilton, understood what was expected of him in the coming months.

In August 1560, the Lords of the Congregation and their supporters, including Hamilton, duly ensured that the Scottish Parliament abolished the jurisdiction of the Pope in Scotland, declared the saying and hearing of Mass illegal, and approved the Calvinist Confession of Faith that had been drawn up by John Knox and his colleagues to establish the doctrine and liturgy of the new Church.

The Reformed Church on Lismore

In their haste to deal with theology, the reformers neglected many of the practical aspects, such as the supply of a Protestant minister for each parish, the role of senior clergy such as bishops in a non-episcopal Church, and what to do about the property of cathedrals, abbeys and priories. Faced with such enormous problems, the early General Assemblies voted to operate on a 'business as usual' basis until they had the opportunity to develop practical guidelines. Bishops were replaced by regional superintendents but all non-reformed clergy were guaranteed two-thirds of their livings for life. Teinds and property were to be retained for Church use, including the establishment of a school in every parish, but in practice much of the property was appropriated by secular landlords.

This policy of 'business as usual' does seem to have operated on Lismore, although, in view of the reforming zeal of Archibald Campbell, the cathedral would have been stripped of any decoration. John Carswell was appointed superintendent of Argyll, and devoted himself to developing a Gaelic version of the reformed Book of Common Order, the first published book in the language (1567), which was important in ensuring that Protestantism took root in Argyll. He also oversaw the introduction of Protestant ministers to Argyll parishes and an improvement in their education (those carrying the title 'Mr' were university graduates). Nevertheless, Bishop Hamilton remained in place until 1580, and was succeeded by four more Protestant bishops up to 1638 when strict Presbyterianism was established in opposition to the attempts by Charles I to impose Anglican liturgy on Scotland. The continuation of the cathedral chapter had been facilitated by James VI's reimposition of bishops in Scotland in 1610 and as late as 1622 a Glenorchy charter was signed by Andrew Boyd, bishop; Adam Boyd, archdeacon; Neil Campbell, chancellor; Dugald Campbell, dean; Mr Colin Campbell, precentor and rector of Cragneis; and the parsons of Knapdale, Lochaw, Kilbride and Kilchalmonell. Bishop Boyd has been credited with setting up the first parish school on Lismore around 1615 and there seems to have been reasonable continuity in elementary education from that time.

The career of Gavin Hammiltoun shows the diocese of Lismore in transition. Probably a relative of Bishop Hamilton, possibly even one of his three sons, Hammiltoun was 'presented' by Duncan Campbell of Glenorchy to the bishop as candidate for the chancellorship of Lismore vacated by Dougall MacGregor around 1570. For the next 50 years he played the dual roles of lawyer to the landowner and chancellor to the dean and chapter of the cathedral. His loyalty to Glenorchy was secured in 1585 by a lifetime grant of an extensive estate of eight merklands in the Loch Tay area with an annual rental of £65 Scots. At his death around 1620, Gavin Hammiltoun's services were rewarded by an annual pension of £60 Scots to his widow, Margaret Fischer, daughter of one of the priests associated with Lismore. Over this period, it was in the interest of the landowner to maintain the outdated arrangements of the old Church to ensure the continuation of legal services and to help in the acquisition of church property. From the 1590s, secular 'writers', such as Gavin's son Patrick Hammiltoun, begin to appear in Glenorchy documents.

In spite of their devotion to the Protestant cause, the Glenorchy family was not slow to exploit the possibilities of the new arrangements by appropriating the teinds of the cathedral: '1570/1 January 15. Tack by Neil Campbell, chanter [precentor] of Lesmoir, with consent of dean and chapter of Kirk of Lesmoir, to Catherine Ruthvene, Lady Glenurquhay, and Patrick Campbell of Achinryr, son of said Catherine and Colin Campbell of Glenurquhay, of teindsheaves of lands pertaining to said chantry, for three years from Beltane next, and so on for three years at a time, for granter's lifetime' (witnessed by Neil Campbell, chanter; Gavin Hammiltoun, chancellor, Archball Conighame, commissar; Mr Donald Carswell; and endorsed by James, Bishop of Argyll). The Glenorchy Campbells succeeded in holding on to one-third of the teinds of Lismore well into the eighteenth century.

Although possession of these rights carried the duty to provide financial support to the Lismore church and clergy, it provided an opportunity to divert resources to secular uses, and to exert pressure on the clergy. Clearly the Reformation did not relieve the clergy of the need to show deference to the landed classes. By the 1630s, Mr Duncan McCalman, the sole 'minister at the kirk of Kilmaluag in Lesmoir' was due a stipend from Sir Colin Campbell of Glenorchy and Sir Donald Campbell of Ardnamurchan of 14 bolls bere, 28 bolls oatmeal and 250 merks Scots, but the church commissioners were recommending that it be increased by 200 merks. As explained in a later section, underfunding of the parish became chronic and, by the 1730s, the minister was complaining that part of his stipend had not been paid for several years.

Although the teinds were quickly alienated, records of legal transactions on Lismore indicate that the cathedral chapter held on to its lands until the 1630s, when Charles I granted Sir James Livingston of Skirling (in Lanarkshire), a member of his personal household, a 57-year lease of the church lands in Argyll, including those on Lismore. There is an undocumented tradition that he occupied Achinduin Castle at this time. Livingston's tenure cannot have survived the execution of the king in 1648 and it appears that the lands of Achinduin, Frackersaig and Craignich reverted to the feudal superior, the Earl of Argyll. However, the short Livingston tenure had an important effect on the MacLeays of Bachuil.

In 1541 the Earl of Argyll was required to surrender his lands to James V so that they could be formally re-granted. In turn, the earl formalised his charters with his own feuars, issuing, in 1544, the oldest surviving charter to the MacLeays, confirming their long-standing role as keepers of the staff of Moluag. However, the charter seems to have reduced their landholding to *half* of Peynabachuille (Pennybachuil) and Peynchallen – in total, a half merkland that was separate from the church lands. With their role as dewars (guardians of a holy relic) under question in the reformed Church, and their feudal superior's lands being ravaged by the royalist forces in the 1640s, the MacLeays appear to have sought the protection of Sir James Livingston and adopted his name (ultimately in the form Livingstone), particularly when travelling outside the Highland area. The MacLeay or Maconlea name appears in Lismore documents for another hundred years at least. For example, John McInlea junior was one of the 22 men from Lismore causing trouble at the Baligrundle mill in 1728. However, by 1745 all of the members of the wider family were using the Livingstone form. It is ironic that alliance with Sir James provided no protection against the greed of Sir Donald Campbell of Ardnamurchan.

Campbell, known for his violent temperament, was an illegitimate son of Campbell of Cawdor, trained for the church and appointed to the deanship of Lismore. His father was assassinated in 1592 at the instigation of the Campbells of Glenorchy and Ardkinglas, who aimed to exploit the vulnerability of the young Earl of Argyll and dominate the Campbell empire. Taking responsibility for pursuing the murderer and his accomplices, Donald Campbell became the principal supporter and counsellor of the earl and this gave him ample scope for his ruthless acquisition of land, including Canna, Ardnamurchan and a substantial portion of Appin centred on Castle Stalker. Some of the land he acquired on Lismore in the 1640s and 1650s (Cloichlea, Kilandrist and Balnagowan) was granted legally by the grateful earl but tradition has it that he also tricked the Livingstones out of part of their holding. Arranging for the skin of the black sheep of Alisrath to be planted in the barn at Bachuil when all of the household were in church listening to his sermon, Campbell accused the Livingstones of sheep stealing and blackmailed them into releasing part of their land to him, leaving them with only 10 to 12 acres. The lost land appears to have included Baligarve and part of the area around Clachan up to the boundary with Killandrist, and he also took the adjacent minister's glebe surrounding the church. Campbell repented on his deathbed in mortal fear of divine retribution, but this did not prevent his Lismore farms from passing to the Campbells of Airds through his granddaughter. The 1751 valuation shows that he also managed to acquire two-thirds of the Lismore 'Chancellary and Chantry' teinds (the original Argyll portion, amounting to £17 0s 7d sterling), with only £8 5s 7d left for the Earls of Breadalbane (Glenorchy).

The Parish in the Seventeenth and Eighteenth Centuries

The reformed parish, generally known as Kilmaluag, was extensive, covering Lismore, Appin, Duror, Glencoe and Kingairloch on the western shore of Loch Linnhe, although the northern part had traditionally been served by ancient churches at Keil in Duror and on Eilean Munde in Loch Leven. Attempts to separate Appin and Duror from Lismore from the 1640s were unsuccessful and the unfortunate parishioners of Kingairloch had to face a hazardous sea crossing until 1895 when they joined the parish of Ardgour. The demands made on the early ministers did not stop at serving such a vast area. Duncan McCalman, vicar in Lismore until he changed to become a Presbyterian in 1638, had to remain on good terms with the Campbell landlords to ensure that he received his salary but they did little in return to ensure that he had the basic necessities for life. With no manse or glebe, he and his successors were obliged to find lodgings where they could on the island. It is hardly surprising that he was frequently absent at his wife's home in Sunart, for which he was censured by the presbytery. Shortly before his death in 1644 his duties extended to acting as military chaplain to the Earl of Argyll.

There were also enormous spiritual challenges. Over the centuries in the West Highlands and Islands there had developed a complex body of religious beliefs incorporating residual pagan elements (fire, sun, nature and landscape worship), reverence towards early Celtic saints such as Brigid (Bride), mainstream Catholic beliefs including strong cults of the Virgin Mary, intense belief in the afterlife and the visitation of ghosts, as well as a good measure of pure superstition. In the West Highlands and Islands there was a particular attachment to St Michael, the patron saint of boats, sailors and horsemen, and many communities celebrated his feast day on 29 September. The devotional material collected by Alexander Carmichael and published at the end of the nineteenth century in *Carmina Gadelica* (Chapter 10) shows that this rich tradition persisted in some areas until long after the Reformation. There were invocations and prayers for the kindling of the house fire and for keeping it alive overnight by 'smooring' with the ashes of the day, for the work in hand, and for nature and the passage of the seasons:

Grian	Sun
Sùil Dhé mhóir,	The eye of the great God,
Sùil Dhé na glòir,	The eye of the God of glory,
Sùil Righ nan slògh.	The eye of the King of hosts,
Sùil Righ nam beò,	The eye of the King of the living,
Dòrtadh oirne	Pouring upon us
Gach òil agus ial,	At each time and season,
Dòrtadh oirne	Pouring upon us
Gu fòill agus gu fial.	Gently and generously.
Glòir dhuit fhéin,	Glory to thee,
A ghréin an àigh.	Thou glorious sun.
Glòir dhuit fhéin, a ghréin,	Glory to thee, thou sun,
A ghnùis Dhé nan dùl.	Face of the God of life.

(Collected and translated by Alexander Carmichael, *Carmina Gadelica*, vol. 3)

The Ocean Blessing brings together many of these preoccupations

Beannachadh Cuain (The Ocean Blessing)

Thi tha chomhnadh nan ard,
Tiurich duinn do bheannachd aigh,
Iomchair leinn air bharr an t-sal,
Iomchair sinn gu cala tamh,
Beannaich ar sgioba agus bat,
Beannaich gach acair agus ramh,
Gach stadh is tarruinn agus rac,
Ar siul-mhora ri crainn ard
Cum a Righ nan dul 'n an ait
Run's gu 'n till sinn dachaidh slan;
Suidhidh mi fein air an stiuir,
Is e Mac De a bheir domh iuil,
Mar a thug e Chalum ciuin,
'N am dha stadh a chur ri siuil.

O Thou who pervadest the heights,
Imprint on us Thy gracious blessing,
Carry us over the surface of the sea,
Carry us safely to a haven of peace,
Bless our boatmen and our boat,
Bless our anchors and our oars,
Each stay and halyard and traveller,
Our mainsails and our tall masts
Keep, O King of the elements, in their
    place
That we may return home in peace;
I myself will sit down at the helm,
It is God's own Son who will give me
    guidance,
As He gave to Columba the mild
What time he set stay to sails.

Mhuire, Bhride, Mhicheil, Phail,
Pheadair, Ghabriel, Eoin a ghraidh,
Doirtibh oirnn an driuchd o'n aird,
Bheireadh oirnn's a chreideamh fas,
Daingnibh sinn's a Charraig Ail,
Anns gach reachd a dhealbhas gradh,
Run 's gu 'n ruigsinn tir an aigh,
Am bi sith is seirc is baigh
Air an nochadh duinn tre ghras;
Chaoidh chan fhaigh a chnoimh 'n ar
    dail,
Bithidh sinn tearuint ann gu brath,
Cha bhi sinn an geimhlibh bais,
Ge do tha sinn do shiol Adh.

Mary, Bride, Michael, Paul,
Peter, Gabriel, John of love,
Pour ye down from above the dew
That would make our faith grow,
Establish ye us in the Rock of rocks,
In every law that love exhibits,
That we may reach the land of glory,
Where peace and love and mercy reign
All vouchsafed to us through grace;
Never shall the canker worm get near
    us,
We shall there be safe for ever,
We shall not be in the bonds of death
Though we are of the seed of Adam.

La Fheill Micheil, La Fheill Mairt,
La Fheill Andrais, bann na baigh,
La Fheill Bride, la mo luaidh,
Tilg an nimhir sios an chuan,
Feuch an dean e slugadh suas;
Le Fheill Paruig, la nam buadh,
Sorchair oirnn an stoirm o thuath,
Casg a fraoch, maol a gruam,
Diochd a gairge, marbh a fuachd.

On the Feast Day of Michael, the Feast
    Day of Martin
The Feast Day of Andrew, band of
    mercy,
The Feast Day of Bride, day of my
    choice,
Cast ye the serpent into the ocean,
So that the sea may swallow her up;
On the Feast Day of Patrick, day of
    power,
Reveal to us the storm from the north,
Quell its wrath and blunt its fury,
Lessen its fierceness, kill its cold.

La nan Tri Righrean shuas,
Ciuinich dhuinne barr nan stuadh,
La Bealltain thoir an driuchd,
La Fheill Sheathain thoir an ciuin,
La Fheill Moire mor nan cliar,
Seachainn oirnn an stoirm o 'n iar,
Gach la's oidhche, gach stoirm is
    fiamh,
Bi thusa leinn, a Thriath nan triath,
Bi fein duinn ad chairt-iuil,
Biodh do lamh air failm as stiuir,
Do lamh fein, a Dhe nan dul,
Moch is anamoch mar is iul,
Moch is anamoch mar is iul.

On the Day of the Three Kings on
    high,
Subdue to us the crest of the waves,
On Beltane Day give us the dew,
On John's Day the gentle wind
The Day of Mary the great of fame,
Ward off us the storm from the west;
Each day and night, storm and calm,
Be Thou with us, O Chief of chiefs,
Be Thou Thyself to us a compass-
    chart,
Be Thine hand on the helm of our
    rudder,
Thine own hand, Thou God of the
    elements,
Early and late as is becoming,
Early and late as is becoming.

(Collected and translated by Alexander Carmichael, *Carmina Gadelica*, vol. 1.)

The new Presbyterian ministers, charged with replacing the mystery of the Mass with the logic of the sermon, with rooting out all traces of superstition and saint worship, and with imposing strict Sunday observance, must have found their task very daunting. On the island, the single-handed minister trying to foster Protestantism faced the persistence of paganism in the form of fire rituals in spring and autumn (common throughout the Highlands until the twentieth century) and the willingness to ascribe life's difficulties to agents from 'the otherworld'. For example, in more than one traditional story, a beautiful *glaistig*, hiding her goatlike lower half with flowing clothes, begs a lift back to Lismore from Kingairloch but exhausts the rower by rowing against him. Mental illness, deformity and disablement were commonly explained in terms of intervention by fairies. Islanders were also reluctant to give up Catholic habits such as rosary chants and the celebration of Christmas, and there was a very communal approach to rites of passage such as the proclamation of banns. The Lismore tradition of all present acting as godparents at baptisms persisted well into modern times. On top of this, the minister played a semi-judicial role, for example being called upon in 1643 to pronounce sentence of excommunication on five island men charged with the murder of John McClaine of Mingarie.

There was also the vexed issue of traffic with the Devil. In a climate of repression of traditional beliefs, there developed across Protestant northern Europe and in the colonies in America the idea that there was an epidemic of witchcraft. In Scotland the flames of persecution were fanned by the enthusiasm of James VI, and there were particular problems on Lismore. The island's 'white witches' had such a reputation that their advice was sought not only on matters of domestic importance but also by the ruling classes. Campbell archives show that the planning of the assassination of Campbell of Cawdor in 1592 involved consultations with Euphrick Ninichol Roy (alias Efric Nichol) and Christian Nicean vic Couil vic Gillespie. There are no traditional accounts of the burning of witches on the island but in 1677 Donald McIlmichael was hanged at Inveraray after a confused confession involving not only the Devil and witches but also fairies. At his trial for theft of livestock, including horses from Balnagowan on Lismore, he admitted consulting the Devil on the discovery and disposal of stolen goods but he also described his attendance at Sabbath dances in a fairy hillock where he played the Jew's harp. His obvious insanity did not protect him from execution. The island horses must have provided a continuing temptation as, in 1718, Duncan MacKendrick in Balnagowan was hanged for the theft of seven horses.

Following the Restoration of Charles II, episcopy was restored throughout Scotland in 1661, and the diocese of Argyll was re-established with the new bishop and chapter now based on the mainland. The parish minister of Kilmaluag, Mr Alexander McCalman, who had taken up his charge in 1660, converted from Presbyterianism and became both parish vicar and Dean of Lismore. As well as the hardships of his predecessors, he also had to face the fact that the cathedral had become a roofless ruin by 1679. McCalman was greatly valued by his parishoners. At the final establishment of a Presbyterian Church of Scotland in 1690 he declined to change back, but continued to serve unofficially for a further 27 years from his base in Appin.

The first Presbyterian minister of the parish under the new arrangements, Dugald Campbell, did not take up his charge until 1719. Taking part in the translation of the Psalms and other liturgy into Gaelic, he helped to maintain the tradition established by John Carswell at the Reformation. However, it would be 30 more years before the choir of the cathedral was remodelled to serve as the parish church and a manse built at Clachan (1749), and a further 11 years before the controlling landowners could be prevailed upon to restore the 10- or 12-acre glebe (Tirfuir Croft and part of the graveyard) and expel the resident squatters. In the meantime, at least one of the ministers, Archibald Campbell, made his own arrangements by taking up a tack for Cloichlea. Curiously, he was also named as one of those cited in 1728 for causing trouble at Baligrundle mill.

Bibliography

Black, R. (ed.) (2005) *The Gaelic Otherworld: Rev. John Gregorson Campbell's Superstitions of the Highlands and Islands of Scotland and Witchcraft and Second Sight in the Highlands and Islands*. Edinburgh: Birlinn.

Campbell, A. (2002) *A History of Clan Campbell. 2. From Flodden to the Restoration*. Edinburgh: Polygon.

Carmichael, A. (1960) *The Sun Dances. Prayers and Blessings from the Gaelic* (selected by A. Bittleston). London: The Christian Community Press.

Cowan, I.B. (1982) *The Scottish Reformation: Church and Society in Sixteenth-Century Scotland*. London: Weidenfeld & Nicolson.

Dawson, J.A.E. (2002) *The Politics of Religion in the Age of Mary, Queen of Scots: The Earl of Argyll and the Struggle for Britain and Ireland*. Cambridge: Cambridge University Press.

M'Lauchlan, T. (ed) (1862) *Dean of Lismore's Book*. Edinburgh: Edmonston & Douglas.

9

9.⚓

1750–1850: An Island in Crisis

During the 1745–6 rebellion, the Dukes of Argyll were able to use their political influence and military resources to keep a firm grip on potential Jacobites in most of Argyll. By raising the Argyll militia (effectively a private army of nearly 3,000 men), and maintaining a chain of garrisons (Kilchurn, Dunstaffnage, Stalker and Inverlochy), they avoided the devastation wreaked by government forces on areas such as Morvern and Appin, which had risen to support the Pretender. As in the 1640s, Lismore was spared, but it could not be protected from the effects of a combination of economic and environmental changes (increased population, rising rents, cattle disease, poor harvests, bankrupting of landlords, the Napoleonic Wars, and finally the potato famine) that were to drive more than a quarter of its people from the island between 1830 and 1850.

Campbell Landlords

By the middle of the eighteenth century, Lismore was still a Campbell island but the balance of power had shifted. The valuation of 1751 shows that the middle slice, which had belonged to Glenorchy until 1734, had been passed on to two grandsons of John Campbell of Barcaldine. Baligrundle, Achnacroish, Killean and Portcharron were now owned by Colin Campbell of Glenure, son of Patrick Campbell of Barcaldine by his second marriage to Lucy, daughter of Cameron of Locheil. The neighbouring townships of Balliveolan (including the northern part of Sailean) and Balimakillichan

Argyllshire Valuation Roll, 1751
(Rents in pounds sterling)

Archd Duke of Argyll
Finknockan	£6	13s	4d
Achindown	£17	16s	4d

John Earl of Breadalbane
for his Chancellary and Chantry tiends of Lismore	£8	5s	7d

Donald Campbell of Airds
Cloichlea	£2	16s	1d
Balimenach and Baligarve	£18	19s	4d
Half Croft Bachil	£0	12s	1d
Killandrist and Crofts	£7	9s	7d
Balnagowan and Crofts	£6	17s	7d
Cornmiln thereof	£0	16s	3d
Deanary tiends of Lismore	£17	0s	7d

Colin Campbell of Glenure
Balligrundle and miln	£17	17s	7d
Achnacroish	£8	13s	7d
Killean	£8	13s	7d
Portcharron	£6	16s	8d

John Campbell of Balliveolan
Balliveolan	£19	19s	10d
Ballimakillichan	£13	3s	8d

Neil Campbell of Dunstaffnage
Kilcheran	£12	1s	4d

John Campbell of Combie
Fiart	£22	3s	10d
Achinard	£11	3s	6d

Archibald Campbell
Frackersaig	£14	12s	2d

Coll McDougall
Craignich	£22	2s	2d

Dugald Campbell
Achuran	£12	0s	

John Campbell
Tirefour	£3	10s	3d
Tirlaggan	£5	5s	3d

Duncan McLea
Half Croft Bachill	£0	8s	4d

(including Portcastle, or Coeffin, and Creckanbreck), had been combined into a single estate and given to John Campbell, cousin of Colin but by an illegitimate line, who lived at Drumavuic on Loch Creran, near Glenure, but opted to call himself Campbell of Balliveolan.

Their main rival on the island and in the scramble for lands of the forfeited Jacobites after Culloden was Donald Campbell of Airds, a descendant of both the Glenorchy and Cawdor Campbells, and factor to the Duke of Argyll until 1787; he built the grand Airds House to replace the cramped accommodation of Castle Stalker. Airds had inherited the Lismore townships acquired by the unscrupulous Donald Campbell of Ardnamurchan, mainly to the north of Glenure's holding (Killandrist, Balnagowan, half of Bachuil and Baligarve) but also Cloichlea to the south-east. Although the Duke of Argyll remained the feudal overlord of the entire island, his direct holding was much reduced as a result of gifts to Ardnamurchan and also by the sale of Fiart and Achanard (to John Campbell of Combie, an entrepreneurial cattle dealer from Loch Aweside), Kilcheran (to Neil Campbell of Dunstaffnage), Frackersaig and Craignich. In 1751 he is recorded as owner of the former church lands of Achinduin in the south-west, and the former Stewart of Appin lands of Finknockan at the north end (extending over the modern farms of Laggan and Park, the peninsula of Alisrath, Port Ramsay and its crofts). The deeds of Park Farm refer to it as 'the Big Park of Finknockan', recalling its ancient role as the place of refuge for cattle when raiders threatened (Chapter 4). The valuation is not helpful in defining the boundary between Finknockan and Achuran, another former Stewart township, owned at this time by Dugald Campbell. The township of Achuran probably included the modern farms of Stronacroibh and Point.

The Argyllshire Valuation Roll shows that the two most valuable farms on the island, with rents greater than £22 each, were Fiart and Craignich in the south-east, reflecting the relative fertility and ease of cultivation of these areas, and the density of population. The value placed on this part of Lismore is further emphasised by the fact that the rent of the more marginal Achanard, much of it on the exposed south-west slopes of Barr Mòr facing Mull, was over £11 – higher than Finknockan, Balnagowan, Achnacroish or Killean. Baligarve (with Balimenach), Achinduin, Baligrundle, and

Balliveolan were intermediate in value: over £15. These comparisons should, however, not be driven too far as the attitudes and policies of the different landowners would have varied. Nevertheless, the modern visitor will find it very difficult to reconcile the emptiness of the south-east quarter of the island with these valuations.

Unlike other parts of Lowland Argyll in the first half of the eighteenth century, there appears to have been no attempt to amalgamate the Lismore township holdings into single farms. Argyll landowners corresponded about Improvement, by which they normally meant driving up productivity by increasing rents, but they were unwilling to bring this about by investment. In some areas of the West Highlands, notably the Breadalbane estates, Islay and Kintyre, rents were rising as early as the 1730s and the 'middlemen' tacksmen were being squeezed out. This resulted in significant emigration, particularly to the Carolinas. However, on Lismore, until the last quarter of the century, the structure of farming was traditional: the (non-resident) owner leased fractions of townships, commonly by verbal agreement, to tenants who cultivated the land in the time-honoured ways with the help of an army of landless cottars. Continuous cropping of cereals (oats and barley) predominated, and both prices and rents were relatively high for the region because of the demand for cereals, not least bere barley for local whisky production.

Although the management of the duke's farms was slightly different, with leases of townships given to tacksmen from the landed classes (for example, Glenure had the tack for Achinduin in 1751 in addition to his own estate on the island), the pattern was effectively the same. The population of the island was dominated by landless cottars and craftsmen, with relatively few small tenants, and ground officers (representing the landlords and keeping the others in order), but society was relatively stable. As long as the tenant paid his rent and refrained from anti-social activities, he could expect to have his short-term tack renewed indefinitely. The cottars were in a more precarious situation: even though they played a central role in providing services to the community as carpenters, joiners, weavers, tailors, shoemakers and merchants, their occupation of property in the townships had no legal basis and they had to leave with the outgoing tenant. For example, tenants leaving Glenure's estate in 1766 agreed 'to remove our selves our wives children cottars goods and gear' and, at any time, cottars could be evicted at will by landlords who, not being resident on the island, had little interest in supporting the wider community. The minister occupied a unique and very arduous position in this society as the only highly educated resident, although elementary education was available for all children who could be spared from manual work. At times it must have been impossible to reconcile his duty for the care and protection of his parishoners with the demands of the landlords and his responsibilities as the effective government official on the island.

The '45 in Argyll

In spite of the ancient and continuing links of kinship between Lismore and Appin, muster lists from the '45 rebellion include only two recruits from the island to the Appin regiment, eventually involving more than 200 men (Stewarts, Carmichaels, MacColls, MacCombies, MacIntyres, MacKenzies and MacLarens), who marched with Charles Stuart throughout the rebellion. They were Sergeant John Stewart, brewer of Craignich, and Donald Livingstone (probably a Livingstone of Bachuil, joining a small group of the name from Morvern, Ballachulish and Perthshire). As elsewhere in Argyll, including Mull and Tiree, the firm hold of the Campbells over society subdued any Jacobite leanings amongst most of their tenants; only Morvern, Ardnamurchan and Appin rose in numbers. For Lismore, two additional factors were important: the island was strongly Presbyterian, and there were Campbell/government garrisons in Dunstaffnage and Castle Stalker keeping the countryside in line throughout the emergency. The brutal burning of Morvern, left unprotected by the rebel forces, by an amphibious government force in March 1746 showed the people of the island what they could have expected if their loyalty had been uncertain.

From the point of view of some of the rebelling clans, this was as much a struggle against the Campbells as against the Hanoverian government, and the Campbell contribution was critical in bringing the emergency to an end. At the outbreak in August 1745, the duke set off for London to play his part at the centre of government, and his cousin, General John Campbell of Mamore, was recalled from Flanders to coordinate the defence of the west. His son was a senior officer in the regular forces commanded by Lord Loudon, who belonged to an Ayrshire branch of the clan. Nearly 3,000 militiamen were mustered and armed in Argyll, gentlemen of the many cadet branches (including Airds, Barcaldine and Baleveolan) rushed to sign up as officers, and they were soon in action repelling the only invasion of Argyll, in November, by MacGregor of Glengyle. Thereafter the area remained outside the conflict.

We know the names of the active Jacobites in 1745–6 because each minister was required to make an official return to the local sheriff, listing the rebels from their parish. Corresponding lists of those joining the government side, for example from Lismore, must have existed, but they are not held in national military archives. They may re-emerge as more estate records are explored. However, it is probably safe to say that a significant number of men, possibly as many as 50, would have been recruited into the company raised by Donald Campbell of Airds, who held a captaincy in the militia. Airds' militiamen were involved in the defence of Argyll against Glengyle, later joining the regular forces of the Duke of Cumberland's army.

The record of the Argyll militia was mixed, including a headlong retreat at Falkirk in January 1746. Because of this and his animus against Highlanders in general, Cumberland considered the militia to be expendable, and sent them ahead throughout his march north. In one skirmish in Keith a party of Argyll militiamen was captured. Barcaldine's brother, although severely wounded, survived, but the sons of Baleveolan and Campbell of Ardchattan were shipped off to France as prisoners of war, returning on exchange in 1747. The Argyll militia went on to play an active part in the Battle of Culloden, where Lismore men would have faced their Appin Regiment neighbours, and the conduct of the militia there finally convinced Cumberland of their worth. After taking part in the disarming of the western seaboard, they were disbanded in August 1746.

The Lismore laird, Colin Campbell of Glenure, also had a mixed record during the emergency as a lieutenant in the regular army under Lord Loudon. The grandson of Sir Ewen Cameron of Locheil, one of the leaders of the rebellion, he found himself fighting against his kinsmen in the defeat at Prestonpans. Later, as the Jacobite army moved north, he was placed in command of a mixed troop of regular soldiers and militiamen deployed to block any advance south through Atholl. Absent on personal business when Lord George Murray captured or killed nearly all of his men, Glenure somehow managed to avoid being court-martialed. He spent the rest of the emergency on the staff of Lord Crawford, who commanded the government troops in Perthshire.

Lismore emerged unscathed in 1746, although the Livingstones of Bachuil claim that their house was burned, but the island was drawn into the aftermath through its involvement with the red-haired Glenure – the Red Fox. Already a landowner and tacksman on Lismore, he had greater ambitions, obtaining the factorship of the forfeited estate of Stewart of Ardsheil as well as two smaller areas in Cameron country north of Ballachulish. Glenure's intention to evict the incumbent Stewart tacksmen from the Ardsheil townships and replace them with Campbells, including his cousin Campbell of Baleveolan, led to his death at the hands of an unknown assassin near Ballachulish in May 1752: the Appin murder. In due course, his younger brother Duncan inherited his lands on Lismore and succeeded him as tacksman of Achinduin.

The Downward Spiral, 1750–90

The decades following Culloden saw an unrelenting struggle between the Campbell landowners and the small tenants on the island. In place of the traditional solidarity among tacksman, tenant and cottar, the landlord now took a commercial view of his land, whereas the tenants lost the informal security of tenure that underpinned feudal society. This, naturally, led to conservatism and resistance to change in the townships, and further estrangement between the two parties.

Increased rents could be justified only if crop yields and/or prices were stable and rising. Because of the relatively high rainfall on Lismore, cereal growing was very demanding and, for sustained improvement in yield, there needed to be extensive changes in crop management and husbandry. These included improved fertility and weed control by the introduction of rotations. Regular sowing of part of the arable land to grass and clover would increase nutrient levels and improve livestock production, with the added benefit of more fertility through their manure. In spite of the fact that the bedrock is limestone, there was also a need for regular liming of soils that had been sown relentlessly to cereals over the centuries.

Changes of this kind were possible under existing rig and furrow cultivation, if all of the tenants agreed to the new approaches, and if the cropped land was enclosed to protect it against grazing livestock. However, any move from the very short-season bere to higher-potential oat and barley crops carried a real risk of crop failure. A systematic approach to the Improvement of the island might have involved: a model farm, showing the benefits of rotations; long-term rationalisation of the land area of the subdivided townships; paid employment to improve the drainage and build enclosing walls; supply of improved seed, varieties and stock; an estate limekiln exploiting the island limestone, which could have had the added benefit of supplying the mainland with much-needed lime (as well as cash income for the landlord). Productivity would also have benefited from investment in barns and byres, if not dwelling-houses.

These ideas were familiar to the ruling elite but they were unwilling to invest the required time, capital and management needed to bring them about. They wanted a rapid return on their capital to fund the costs of increasingly expensive lifestyles. Society was polarising rapidly and there was the additional problem for Lismore that the landowners were physically distant and not directly involved with the island community and its welfare. Their normal approach – increasing rents at the expiry of leases and hoping to attract more entrepreneurial tenants by competition – destabilised society and resulted in widespread arrears of rent. For example, from the 1770s to the 1790s, the tenants at Achinduin were chronically in arrears and in 1798 they appealed to the minister, Rev. Donald McNicol, to intervene to prevent the township being let to an outsider at a much higher rent. The Barcaldine archives of the period include numerous warnings of evictions across the island, and the instability is illustrated by the number of small tenants, whose families had lived for generations in one part of the island, applying to other landlords for tacks. It is no wonder that, when Glenure started to plan the enclosure of his own landholding on the island, he met with active resistance from the people. In his return for the First Statistical Account in 1791, Rev. McNicol judged that there had been little progress in agriculture: in his opinion, the principal impediment to Improvement was the lack of coal to burn lime, and only the gentlemen of the area had tried ryegrass, clover and turnips.

A further complication was the rapid rise in population. Across the West Highlands population levels had been held in check by warfare and raiding (most recently the devastations of the 1640s and 1746) and by high mortality during years of famine, which could have been as frequent as one year in three. Apart from a reduction in warfare and lawlessness, the factor that now affected survival rates across the region was the arrival of the potato. At first scorned in the West Highlands as a sustaining food, the potato came into its own after the famine of 1780, when a series of severe winters and wet summers (caused by the coincidence of El Niño years with a major volcanic eruption on Iceland) ruined crops across northern Europe. As noted by Thomas Pennant, even in normal years in the 1770s, the diet and health of the islanders were dominated by food shortages:

> The inhabitants in general are poor, are much troubled with sore eyes, and in the spring are afflicted with a costiveness [constipation] that often proves fatal. At that season all their provisions are generally consumed; and they are forced to live on sheeps' milk, boiled, to which the distemper is attributed.

Tolerant of poor acid soils in wet climates, the potato could generate the calories needed by the cottar's family on a much smaller area than that needed by oats, and there was no need to carry grain to the mill. This was also the time when inoculation began to reduce the scourge of smallpox.

With decreased infant mortality and increased longevity, the population of the area began to climb. The 1692 muster shows than there were around 100 'fencible men' on Lismore, indicating that the total number of islanders was perhaps around 500. By the time of the First Statistical Account (1791), it had risen to over 1,100, and the peak, at nearly 1,500, was probably reached around the time of the 1831 census. Confusingly, in a letter to

Thomas Pennant in May 1774, Donald McNicol estimated that 'the number of Souls in Lismore alone is about 1500' and John Knox made the same claim in 1786. There are reports of numbers reaching 1,800 between 1810 and 1830 but these must have included the Kingairloch people. The first fully reliable population count, including only those resident on the island on 6 June 1841, is 1,148. There are problems even with this figure because it indicates that there were 80 more males than females, a disparity which is only partly explained by the greater numbers of surviving boys (Chapter 10). It is possible that women were absent from the island, employed as gutters by the early summer herring fisheries.

Whatever the precise number of people trying to make their living on Lismore in the late eighteenth century, it is clear that pressures on the land and resources of the island were growing. With a limited number of tenancies available, there were few prospects for younger sons and more of them were surviving. Across the region, emigration was seen as the solution. It is impossible to know how many people moved permanently to the mainland at this time, but there were expanding opportunities on Improving farms and in the mills of the Lowlands. What is known is that, between 1770 and 1800, there was a significant movement of islanders to the well-established West Highland settlements in the Carolinas. Donald Black (34), with his wife Janet (34) and four children (Christian, Ann, Ewen and Duncan), and Archibald Carmichael (26), with his wife Mary (26) and daughter Catherine, joined a party of 136 emigrants, mostly from Appin and Glenorchy, who sailed on the *Jupiter of Larne* in spring 1775, reaching Wilmington, North Carolina, on 9 April. Archibald was moving to join his brother Duncan, who had been in America for two years, and in 1792, after the War of Independence was over, another brother, Donald (Daniel) and his family, from Cloichlea, joined them. During the same period, at least one other trio of Carmichael brothers and their dependents emigrated to the Carolinas. However, it is unlikely that the total number of emigrants from Lismore to the USA in this period exceeded 100.

Knowledge of the pattern of emigration from the island in the early nineteenth century is now growing, through the number of descendants seeking information about their origins through the Comann Eachdraidh Lios Mòr (The Lismore Historical Society).

Judging from the population losses in the 1830s, *before* the major clearance by James Cheyne, there must have been significant emigration to the colonies and to the industrial centres before 1841. Surviving letters home to the island show that there was a thriving colony of Lismore families (McDonalds, Grahams, Blacks, Buchanans and McColls from Baleveolan, Fiart and Frackersaig) in Cape Breton Island, Nova Scotia from the 1820s. Lismore McColls and McCorquodales settled in Ontario around the same time. In the 1840s, new emigrants were being advised to go to the Midwest of the USA or to Australia as the limitations of life in Cape Breton became clearer. Up to this point, the emigrants were mainly voluntary, financing their removal and establishment in their new life from savings. Many were joining family members who had pioneered the way. Their chances of success in a new life were much better than of those forcibly removed in the decades after 1830.

Early Tourists

From the 1770s, with the events of 1745–6 fading behind a romantic mist generated by James McPherson's *Ossian*, the West Highlands and Islands became a favourite area for adventurous tourists, whose journals provide insights into the living conditions of the day. Most of these tourists followed Samuel Johnson and James Boswell in passing Lismore by on the way to or from more celebrated sites between Mull and Skye. However, Thomas Pennant, on the second of his detailed fact-finding trips in 1772, did manage to spend a few hours on Lismore, visiting the 'Danish Fort' (Tirfuir Broch) and the church. Unfortunately for him, the Rev. Donald McNicol was away from the island that day but later, in 1774, he wrote twice to Pennant, providing a mass of factual information. So much of this is included in Pennant's journal that it is difficult to disentangle his own impressions but he was clearly unimpressed by the health of the people (see page 121) or by the state of the island farms:

> The chief produce of the land is bere and oats. The first is raised in great quantity, but abused by being distilled into whisky. The crops of oats are generally applied to the payment of rent; so that

the inhabitants are obliged for their subsistence annually to import much meal.

The ground has in most parts the appearance of great fertility, but is extremely ill-managed, and much impoverished by excess of tillage, and neglect of manure.

About a hundred head of cattle are annually exported, which are at present remarkably small ... Horses are in the island very short-lived. They are used when about two or three years old: and are observed soon to lose all their teeth. Both they and the cows are housed during winter, and fed on straw.

He did not repeat McNicol's report that

Our climate here is bad, I mean wet, & tho we have a flattering appearance of corn early in the season, the great falls of rain in July & August destroys all, & frequently make our crops turn out to small acct. in the end.

There were also official tours of the area. In 1786 John Knox travelled through the Highlands and Islands in the service of the British Society for Extending Fisheries and Agriculture. He devotes less than two published pages to Lismore and, commenting on the need to import meal and to rely heavily on milk, he suggests that:

If this be the situation of a spot naturally fertile, we may easily conceive the distress of the parish, of which Lismore forms only a very small part.

Later celebrated literary tourists such as the Wordsworths and Coleridge (1803) and Walter Scott (1814) passed by without visiting.

Campbell of Baleveolan and his Tenants

With time, the small people learned to subvert the wishes of the landlords. Towards the end of the 1790s, Donald Campbell of Baleveolan instructed his lawyer, A.R. Bell in Inveraray, to arrange for the removal of most of his tenants in the townships of Baleveolan and Balimakillichan. A series of surviving letters from Bell to Campbell shows that the tenants mounted their resistance in the sheriff court by combining to engage their own legal support. As Baleveolan's agreements with most of the tenants had been verbal, he imagined that eviction would be straightforward. However, since he had demanded cash grassums at entry, the court ruled that, if confirmed, these would be equivalent to written leases. Most of the agreements had one more year to run, but Donald and John McGlashan and John Black had five-year leases in the township of Baleveolan. On 15 May 1798, when it was already too late to force eviction that year, Bell advised Campbell to sign a statement on oath denying that these agreements existed. However, on 15 June, Bell reported that the agents for the tenants had convinced the court in Inveraray that Campbell must appear in person to take the oath, and that he could avoid this only if he could produce a 'surgeon's certificate' to confirm that he was too ill to travel.

When Bell applied for a 'decreet of removal' of the tenants in spring 1799, they lodged a written defence that Campbell had agreed verbally that they could remain for a further year. Under the circumstances this seems unlikely, but the process was again delayed and it was not until 25 May that Bell was able to report that the sheriff substitute had overturned their defence and issued the decreet, to be served on the tenants as soon as possible by a sheriff officer. The state of the relationships can be gauged by the lawyer's advice that a 'party of the military' might be required if the officer failed to secure agreement to their removal. Clearly, the landed classes were worried that revolutionary ideas from France might be infecting the common people of Scotland. It is not clear how many were cleared out by the end of the 1799 growing season but, by resisting the process, they had extended their leases by at least a year. Meanwhile, John McLachlan and the widow and son of John Black in Balimakillichan pointed out that their names had not been included in the list for removal on Whit (15 May) 1798, requiring Bell to go back to court to complete the business.

The ability of the tenants to use the legal processes to their benefit was not yet exhausted, because John McKeich, one of those evicted in 1799, was back farming on Campbell's land in 1800 as a subtenant. As this was judged to be a new contract, the court required that a further notice of removal would have to be issued. In parallel with this struggle, Campbell was also trying to evict the

MacKenzie brothers early from the quarry on Balimakillichan, for which they had a written lease up to 1799. By the incompetence of Campbell and Bell (mistakes in dates and not noticing that there was a third name on the tack), and the care of their own agent (another MacKenzie), the brothers were able to remain in place until 1800.

Although it is satisfying to discover that the tenants were far from compliant, there were no winners in this game. The tenants had been treated with contempt by a landlord who withheld security of tenure and accused them of lying in court. Several of them were evicted in due course. The case of John McGlashan was particularly poignant. Previously evicted from Achnacroish, he wrote to Campbell of Barcaldine for help, saying that he had 'not a place to put my head in'. On the other hand, Campbell of Baleveolan had been obliged to lay out considerable expense in lawyers' fees and, at the end of more than three years of litigation, he had failed to clear the land for Improvement. By April 1801, he seems to have given up the struggle, having neglected to provide Bell with a list of evictions for the year. As we shall see, there were still 14 tenants on the Baleveolan estate as late as 1851.

Campbell of Combie and the Clearance of Achanard

The last quarter of the eighteenth century witnessed a catalogue of bankruptcies among Argyll landowners, whose lifestyles could not be supported by the modest incomes from their estates. These included Campbell of Barcaldine, who was forced to sell out to his half-brother Duncan Campbell of Glenure. The Campbells of Combie (variously Comby, Camby, Claycombie) were also in trouble. John Campbell, a small landowner, cattle breeder and dealer from Lochaweside, had prospered in the years after the rebellion, accumulating land, including the Lismore townships listed in the 1751 valuation (page 114). His son, David, was deeply involved in the movement for improvement of agriculture, advising the Duke of Argyll on cattle breeding. As factor to the Dukes of Sutherland for several years around 1800, he arranged for the exchange of bulls between Dunrobin and Inveraray, and he was directly involved in the organised emigration of tenants from Assynt.

Probably in response to the series of disastrous harvests in the early 1780s, which revealed how marginal much of the arable cropping in the West Highlands could be, Combie enclosed the Lismore township of Achanard, laying it down to grass, and subdividing it with drystone dykes to manage grazing. In the late 1780s, most of the Achanard people were 'turned away', leaving room for one, later two tenants. Out of the population of the island, the number of people cleared must have been modest, probably no more than 10 families. They included John McKillip, who is recorded in 1789 as seeking 'half a merk of Achindown' to support his family; by 1793 he was living in Kilcheran.

Almost immediately, with the start of nearly 25 years of war with Revolutionary and Napoleonic France, demand for agricultural products rose sharply and prices soared. The navy, alone, required huge quantities of meat to be salted. Nationally, grain prices doubled between 1790 and 1815, and reached unprecedented levels around 1800, up to four times the normal market price, owing to poor harvests. The consequences for the urban and landless poor were very serious and, even in Oban, there were riots in 1796 when a local merchant tried to export two cargoes of bere by sea. In the countryside the opportunities were seized by landowners, and it has been estimated that, between 1790 and 1820, rents on Lismore tripled from 10s to 30s per acre.

Surprisingly, these increases held off Combie's creditors for only a short time and in 1808 he drew up an entail in favour of his son Charles to ensure that some of his property, including his land on Lismore (now including Fiart, Achanard and Craignich), could not be sold. David Campbell died in 1814, the family fortunes soon collapsed, and in 1817 Charles Campbell was forced to sell up all of his unentailed land, losing even the family home. Later, in the 1830s, he tried to sell his remaining estates to the Earl of Breadlbane and a wealthy lawyer, James Cheyne, but because of the entail there was an appeal against the sale by other members of the family and it was not until 1841 that the House of Lords judged that the entail was flawed. The sale of Fiart, Achanard and Craignich to Cheyne was completed in 1842.

Meanwhile there had been developments at Achanard. The parish baptism records show that, from around 1810, families began to move back into the township from the neighbourhood.

In spite of considerable turnover, up to around 1835 there were at least six or seven households, presumably mostly cottars seeking land in a very crowded island: an estate map of 1815 confirms the existence of several small patches of cultivated land on the east-facing slope. By the late 1830s, the people were dispersing to the surrounding townships, leaving a single shepherd and his family by 1841.

Cheyne is remembered as the ruthless clearer of the people from the south-east quarter of the island. The Campbells of Combie have been treated more gently by history. At the age of 73, Duncan McDonald told the 1883 Napier Commisioners that Combie had helped his tenants to improve their cattle stock by introducing fresh bulls and providing both summer and winter grazing. Nevertheless, in terms of clearance, the Campbells of Combie had shown the way at Achanard.

Other Sources of Livelihood: Linen, Whisky, Lime and Shipwrecks

Lismore tenants and cottars in the seventeenth and eighteenth centuries living at the subsistence level were effectively self-sufficient. They fed themselves from the land and the sea, and clothed and shod themselves from the wool, flax and leather produced on the island. As we shall see in the next chapter, there were some specialist craftsmen, such as the Connell and MacDonald families of boat builders, but most spinning, weaving, knitting, tailoring and cobbling was carried out in the townships and paid for by barter and exchange.

Encouraged by the establishment of the Board of Trustees for Fisheries, Manufactures and Improvement in Scotland (which provided grants for the growing and processing of flax) in 1720, and the British Linen Company (of which the Duke of Argyll was a leading member) in 1746, the textile industry across Scotland developed commercially, with linen exports contributing significantly to the economy of the country. During the second half of the eighteenth century, linen spinning and weaving enterprises, mainly using imported flax, spread through Argyll, particularly Cowal and Islay. These were based on home-workers, paid in cash, but it was usual to establish spinning schools to train women to achieve the high standards needed for fine linen.

The development on Lismore was unusual for Argyll in that flax growing and processing, as well as spinning and weaving, were encouraged. Early in 1761, Duncan Campbell of Glenure had secured funds from the Board to provide seed for farmers and training in processing the crops; to support the setting up of a spinning school on the island; and to supply the necessary spinning wheels and reels, on the understanding that he would subsidise the enterprise from his own pocket. Glenure lost no time in getting started. His records show that from 1761 the townships of Achnacroish, Baleveolan, Balimakillichan, Baligrundle, Balnagowan, Craignich, Fiart, Killean, Kilcheran and Portcharron were supplying flax for processing and that, with the use of fresh seed each year, the quality of the fibre was good. An itinerant 'flaxdresser' was brought in to show how the fibres should be recovered by retting (soaking the crop in water), bruising or scutching with a wooden swingle, and heckling (combing) in preparation for spinning. In the first season he earned over £4 for 56 stone of heckled flax.

Anticipating financial support, Glenure invested £20 of his own money in erecting a building at Killean to house the spinning school. On 11 March 1761, the Board distributed a printed advertisement for the establishment of the school and the employment of a spinning mistress. Attracted by the promise of eight weeks of training, maintenance (1s 6d per week), prizes for good work, and a spinning wheel to continue the work when they returned home, 31 scholars attended between November 1761 and January 1762, under the guidance of Janet MacArthur. The school reached its target of 40 pupils for the second eight-week session in the late summer of 1762. The 14 girls from Lismore would probably not have required accommodation, although for Janet Mclean and Sarah McIntyre, the walk from and to Achinduin and Finknockan would have made it a very long day. The others were drawn from neighbouring Lorn, from Ardchattan to Glenure, Ardsheal and Shuna. A wheelwright, Patrick MacMartin, was established at Achnacroish, with Board funding, to supply the spinning wheels and reels needed for the school and other users.

In his 1769 petition to the Board for further support, Glenure reported that the linen industry was well established on the island, with surplus yarn and finished linen (probably woven at Portcharron) being sold at local markets. Although he was continuing to supply fresh seed, some flax raisers were still using their own saved seed, to the detriment of the finished yarn. However, his opinion was that the main obstacle to further expansion was the lack of a lint mill to mechanise the processing of the crop. Because the freeing of the fibres from the retted flax by hand was both arduous and inefficient, he had invested in a 'Dutch Break' and one of the 'new foot scutchers', but his experience with these convinced him that a mill, where the retted flax could be fed between rolling drums, was necessary.

Whether or not additional funds were provided, sometime after 1770 a lint mill was built below the corn mill at Balnagowan, powered by the burn running out of the loch. This initiative evoked jealousy amongst the neighbours, and both Campbell of Dunstaffnage and Campbell of Combie threatened to interfere with the water supply. However, any stimulus to the local economy was to be short-lived, and it was effectively over by 1791 when, in the First Statistical Account, Rev. Donald McNicol stated that 'a little flax' was grown on Lismore. By 1841, when the expansion of textile manufacturing and the importation of cheap cotton had destroyed the cottage linen industry in Scotland, Rev. Gregor McGregor expressed his opinion that the establishment of manufacturing would be beneficial for the island.

Although the Board of Trustees for Fishing, Manufactures and Improvement was also involved in establishing fishing harbours and communities in several places along the west coast, there is no record of the development of Port Ramsay in its archives. During his 1786 survey, Knox noted that:

> At the north-east end of Lismore, there is a small island, which defends a bay, sufficiently extensive for all the purposes of fisheries and coasting business. The benefits of a port and market, both to the natives of this island, and the shores upon the Linnhe Loch, must appear obvious to any person who has the map or chart before him.

Until further research clarifies the position, it seems that Port Ramsay was set up in the second half of the eighteenth century by the proprietor, the Duke of Argyll, to exploit the short-lived herring boom in the area. The priority to be given to fishing is supported by the fact that each holding was associated with a very modest croft and limited common grazing. There is some archaeological evidence that the original houses were built end-on to the sea and that the present row of mortared cottages with slate roofs dates from a rebuilding of the entire settlement around 1850, when its economy finally took off (Chapter 10).

There was also the possibility of wage earning for men in the limestone and lime industries. The existence of shallow pits next to piles of limestone rubble in several parts of the island shows that, before the more commercial approach, there was small-scale lime burning in 'clamps' for local use. Rev. Donald McNicol reported in 1791 that 'burning of lime for sale has been begun by adventurers in Lismore and Appin', but the enterprise was limited by the price of coal, inflated by heavy taxation. The first substantial lime kilns were built to support the Roman Catholic Highland seminary, which was based at Kilcheran from 1801 to 1829, although the kilns appear to have operated up to 1840. Another quarry opened on Eilean nan Caoraich in 1808, to provide limestone to be burned elsewhere for building work on the Caledonian Canal, and kilns were established at Sailean by 1826 (probably earlier) and Park by 1830. The impacts of these quarries and kilns on the local economy, including the encouragement of coastal shipping based at Port Ramsay, are considered in the next chapter.

Other legal ways of increasing the cash income of the townships were through harvest labour in the Lowlands and fish gutting during the early summer herring fisheries on the west coast, but there is no way of estimating the extent of seasonal migration of islanders, particularly young women. There was also a growing interest in the breeding of working horses for sale on the mainland. However, what probably did save many of the people of the island, as on the other arable island of Tiree, from utter destitution between 1780 and 1840 was small-scale illicit distillation of whisky, which was produced from island bere and sold for cash.

We have seen that part of the rents of townships on Lismore was traditionally paid in whisky, and there were no restrictions on the production of spirits for domestic use. However, towards the end of the eighteenth century, the government began to take greater control, with the intention of increasing the tax revenue by encouraging large-scale distillation. Heavy duties were introduced, and in 1786 stills of capacity under 40 gallons were completely outlawed. This had the opposite effect, in part because the 'industrial' product, made partly from unmalted grain to reduce malt taxation, was inferior in quality to much of the whisky produced in the Highlands and Islands. Illicit distilling and widespread smuggling of the product prospered to the extent that legal distilleries in Argyll went out of business. During the Napoleonic Wars, landlords were particularly annoyed that their tenants were paying rents in cash when they would have preferred to receive grain, which they could have traded at inflated prices. Aware that their livelihoods were at stake, communities united to oppose the revenue patrols, and the ensuing violence resulted in the deployment of military escorts. The magnitude of the activity can be gauged from the fact that prosecutions in the Highlands peaked at 14,000 in 1823.

Illicit stills were normally operated well away from inhabited areas, where the smoke and odour would be obvious, on a quiet part of the coast where the product could be collected by the whisky smugglers. According to John MacCulloch, whose letters to Sir Walter Scott give detailed descriptions of life in the West Highlands in the 1820s, Lismore was 'one of the most noted seats of illicit distillation' but, of the many illicit stills that must have existed, only two sites are still recognised today. Nothing remains above ground of the activity above the cliffs to the west of Baleveolan, but the well-engineered path down the steep Sloc an Eitheir (Boat Gulley) shows where the whisky could have been carried down to one of the few places on that rugged and secluded coast where a small boat could put in. It is likely that the site of a still in a cleft in the east coast near Baileouchdarach is celebrated in MacCulloch's patronising description of the destruction by a revenue patrol of an enterprise that was probably essential to the survival of the community:

> The morning being fine, I directed the vessel to stand along the north side of Lismore, and, taking the boat, rowed close in shore, under the shadow of the land; now rounding a promontory, now crossing some little bay interspersed with rocks separated by stripes of barley and potatoes, resembling the allotments of infantile gardens, in which, in our youngest days, we used hourly to watch the tedious progress of obstinate cress and more obstinate radishes. Here and there a stray cow was seen pondering over the sea weed that skirted

the tide mark; but, excepting the scream of the gull that flew aloft, or the chatter of a tern as it flitted threatening round our boat, all was silence. Like Palinurus, I was nodding at the helm, when I was roused by a sudden exclamation. 'A Still, a Still!' was the cry, 'pull for your lives, my boys.' Opening my eyes, I immediately perceived the cause of this uproar. Beneath a rock, close by the edge of the water, was burning a bright and clear fire, near which sat an old man and a young girl, with two or three casks scattered about. An iron crook, suspended on some rude poles, supported a Still; and the worm passed into a tall cask, into which fell a small stream from the summit of the rock behind. Two or three sturdy fellows were lounging about; while the alchemist in chief sat over the fire, in the attitude of Geber or Paracelsus waiting for the moment of projection. A rough shed, erected under another rock, seemed to contain some tubs and casks; nor could any thing be more picturesque than this primitive laboratory, or more romantic than the whole scene. But I could only take a glance of these arrangements. Before the boat was well in sight, an universal scream was set up; away ran the girl to some cottages which were perched on the cliff, and down came men, women and children, hallooing, scolding, swearing, and squalling, in all the unappreciable intonations of a Gaelic gamut. One snatched up a tub, another a cask; the still-head was whipt up by a sturdy virago, the malt was thrown out, the wash emptied; but, in the mean time, my men had jumped out into the water and were mixed pell-mell with the operators; scrambling over the rocks, and dashing about among the waves like ducks at the sound of a gun. A chase took place on one side after the Still-head, and as the exciseman was the most swift footed, the chemist dropt his burden and betook himself to his heels. The women stuck fast to their casks and tubs, kneeling, praying, scolding, and screaming; and here the battle raged, as battles are wont to rage when the fair sex is armed against the ruder one, with the three-fold weapons of nails and tongue and tears. But the chief brunt of the war took place at the Still. Though the head had been carried off at the first brush, and the fire kicked out, the cauldron was so hot that the combatants who on each side contested for it, could not hold it long; and as the first possessor of the scalding prize burned his fingers, it fell to the ground, to be again snatched up by some one of the opposed party. At length one of the Chemists seized it effectually; and, flinging it out with a vigorous arm, it fell into the sea. It should have perished in the waters; but, unfortunately the liquor had run out in the contest, and falling with its mouth downwards, it floated, to the great horror of the smugglers, and the delight of the opposed exciseman; who, dashing at it over head and ears, like a Newfoundland dog, rescued it from drowning, and brought it ashore in triumph. In two short minutes the battle was won, and the spoils secured; much sooner indeed than you will read this account of it. But there was little value in all the plunder; which consisted only in the Still and its head. The distillation of the whisky was unfortunately but just commenced; and the little that had run, was overset, to prevent it from falling into the hands of the enemy. What else the excisemen might have destroyed was emptied by the people themselves at the opening of the campaign. I thought that enough had been done, both for glory and for the picturesque; and entreated that they might be allowed to solace themselves in the best manner they could, with the empty casks. I even asked for the restoration of the Still to the poor wretches, who seemed at length quite discomfited and melancholy; but that, unfortunately, was against the law. The rest of the plunder was however given up; but I believe that my arguments had but a small share in effecting this surrender. One of the girls, who was very pretty, fell on her knees to the seaman who had the principal charge, and as he was a handsome good-humoured fellow himself, he could not resist her entreaties. So the lassie wiped her eyes, threw back her long hair with her fingers, and beauty, as usual, gained all that remained to be won of this hard-fought day. We parted in better humour than we began, and returned to the Cutter in triumph, bearing aloft on the prow, like Harold the dauntless, the battered trophies. Thus passed the Battle of the Still; and the shores of Lismore again subsided into peace, as the sounds of conflict were hushed, and the dashing of the oars retired upon the breeze.

Distilling played a major part in the economy of the island between 1790 and 1840, with activity falling away due to the lower price and improved quality of bulk whisky from licensed distilleries in Kintyre and Islay, increased intensity of surveillance from customs officers, and the declining population on the island. As in other areas of the West Highlands, small stills probably continued to operate for many more years and, over the period, there was local demand for the product. The First Statistical Account in 1791 mentions seven or eight public houses on the island, some associated with the ferries to Appin, Kingairloch and Mull and, although the number had fallen by 1841, Rev. Gregor McGregor was not pleased to report the existence of 'several other little dram shops, which are by no means necessary'.

In earlier centuries, the inhabitants would have benefited from the salvage of occasional shipwrecks on the many skerries and reefs around the coast. Although the Lismore lighthouse was not built until 1833, relatively few productive wrecks are recorded in the eighteenth century, but there were two in the 1740s. In the winter of 1742–3 the *London*, carrying 700 hogsheads of tobacco and 90 tonnes of iron, went aground on Creag Island, the most southerly of the Kilcheran Islands (Plate 1b). There was apparently no loss of life and the owner, John Saunders, tried to enlist the help of Airds and Glenure in saving the stranded ship and its valuable cargo, which may actually have been contraband. Clearly, this was unsuccessful as, later in the year, Duncan Campbell was writing from Achnacroish to complain that Captain Andrew Glesgow, who had bought the salvage rights, had not paid him for six weeks of shipbreaking. Officially, most of the tobacco was now fit only for use as manure, but it is difficult to imagine that Lismore pipes were not supplied for many months of that year. Around the same time, a ship carrying French wine was wrecked on Eilean Dubh. Details of this wreck are difficult to trace but it is well known in the area because of the number of salvaged bottles which have found their way into local collections.

James Cheyne and the Clearance of Kilcheran, Baligrundle and Fiart

The son of a wealthy bookseller in Edinburgh, James Auchinleck Cheyne (1793–1853) was educated in the law and achieved the elite status of Writer to the Signet (the society of solicitors in Edinburgh) in 1818. He also trained in accountancy and was a pioneer in the insurance business, becoming manager of the Life Insurance Company of Scotland in 1832. He was a landowner, by inheritance, in Fife (Kilmaron), near Linlithgow (Woodcockdale) and in the Borders (Oxendean), where he was a justice of the peace. Judging by his membership of the Highland and Agricultural Society, and his election to fellowship of the Royal Society of Edinburgh in 1839, he must have been exposed to the current ideas about agricultural Improvement. He certainly permitted himself to be quoted in Blackwoods Magazine of 1850 as an expert on cattle prices and breeding.

After Kilcheran was vacated by the Roman Catholic seminary in 1829 it was acquired in 1833 by Duncan Campbell of Barcaldine, but his finances were soon in crisis and he sold not only Kilcheran but also all of the former Glenure lands to Cheyne in 1845. James Cheyne was now in possession of at least a quarter of the island, including Baligrundle, Achnacroish, Killean, Tirlaggan and Portcharron as well as Achanard, Fiart, Kilcheran and Craignich. He made Kilcheran House his home around 1850, modifying the original seminary buildings. Farming was in deep depression, as the demand for, and prices of, grain and meat had not recovered from the ending of the Napoleonic Wars. Cheap food from North America started to flood the British market, improvements in transport undermined the role of Lismore as a local supplier of grain, a severe epidemic of disease decimated West Highland cattle herds in 1836, and the potato famine of 1846–7 would undermine the ability of the islanders to feed themselves.

Confident in his wealth and position, Cheyne may well have enjoyed the challenge of turning round the agriculture of Lismore. It was clear that the future lay in improved grass and livestock production rather than arable farming, and we know something of Cheyne's tactics to bring this about from testimonies collected on Lismore by the Napier Commission many years later in 1883. Beginning his campaign in Kilcheran, he changed the conditions of the verbal leases to tenants. Over a few years (probably two to five) the tenant was to sow part of his arable land down to ryegrass and clover until the whole area was improved grassland. The tenant was permitted to use the sown land for hay and grazing until the process was complete, and then he and his family were summarily evicted to make way for the landlord's livestock. In the time of the seminary, Bishop Chisholm had tried to stimulate the local economy at Kilcheran, setting up the first large-scale lime kilns on the island. By 1841, although there were only three farmers with four families of cottars, Kilcheran was a thriving community of 100 people, supporting a public house, carpenters, wrights and weavers. However, by 1851, under Cheyne's management, most of the land was farmed by a grieve hired from Fife with a team of ploughmen, nearly half of the people of the community (six family units) had disappeared, and John McColl was the last representative of local tenants, farming 30 acres. With the eventual amalgamation of the township into one farm, without cottars, the demand for services declined and the township had dwindled to 28 in 1861.

Meanwhile, Cheyne had turned his attention to Baligrundle, the next township to the north. By 1851 all four tenants had been removed and replaced by a shepherd, and the progressive removal of all of the people on the township meant that in 1861 the shepherd and his widowed sister-in-law were the sole residents where there had previously been nine families and 44 people. The relentless process, in which Cheyne must have been encouraged by the miseries of the potato famine of 1846–7, continued to Fiart. This township (including Point of Fiart, now Dalnarrow) had been the most productive on the island at the 1751 valuation, supporting six farming tenants in 1841. These had been reduced to three in 1851, but, ten years later, the community of around 40 (eight or nine families) had entirely disappeared, to be replaced by two shepherds, one brought in from Lanarkshire. Any plans that Cheyne may have had for further clearance on his lands were curtailed by his death in 1853.

The tenants did not all go quietly. In the summer of 1843, the death of Archibald McColl, one of the farmers in Baligrundle, offered an early opportunity for Cheyne to clear the McColl family but it appears that his 27-year-old son, Malcolm, resisted the attempt of the police to serve notice of removal – the crime of 'deforcement'. On 26 July, a warrant for his arrest was issued by the sheriff substitute and a party of five, led by Donald MacDonald, police constable in Oban, descended on the McColl home in Baligrundle, apprehended Malcolm and marched him off to Achnacroish, where their boat was lying. However, they underestimated the solidarity of the Lismore community. Malcolm McColl (another Malcolm, 42, mason in Tirlaggan), Duncan Connell (27, farmer's son in Balnagowan) and Donald McLachlan (22, joiner and boat builder in Balnagowan)

> did all and each or one or more of them … near the heights above the Bay of Achnacroish … in concert with a great number of other persons amounting to fifty or sixty or thereby wickedly and feloniously obstruct & deforce Donald MacDonald in the execution of the … warrant knowing him to be an officer of the law then engaged in the execution of his duty, and this they did by pulling … Malcolm McColl from the grasp of … Donald MacDonald and his assistants … and by threat of personal violence to Donald MacDonald and his assistants … and by other violent and riotous

conduct by all which or part thereof the said Malcolm McColl was
rescued from the custody of Donald MacDonald.

The Minutes of the Argyllshire Constabulary Committee indicate
that the forces of law and order were outraged at this behaviour.
On 27 September, the procurator fiscal, in person, arrived on the
island, supported by a superintendent and ten police officers, and
took the three ringleaders prisoner, sending them away successfully
to Inveraray. Later in the day they tried to arrest a further man
(not named but probably the original Malcolm McColl) but the
party was assaulted by the local residents and he escaped. McColl,
Connell and McLachlan had to wait until 2 December, when they
were found guilty of deforcement and sentenced to a further 60
days of imprisonment in Inveraray Prison. In spite of their criminal
records, they appear to have returned to normal life on the island:
McColl was farming in Killean in 1851 and labouring in Craignich
in 1861; Connell remained working at Balnagowan until 1871; and
McLachlan, originally from Mull, reappeared as a ship carpenter
in Port Ramsay in 1861. However, Malcolm McColl and his family
in Baligrundle disappear from view after 1843.

Allan McDougall and the Improvement of Baleveolan

A collection of 87 letters preserved at Bachuil House shows that,
at the time that Cheyne was evicting all his tenants, the factor
for Baleveolan and Balimakillichan was taking a very different
approach. Peter Campbell, grandson of the Donald Campbell
who we have seen harassing his tenants in the 1790s, married
Ann McDougall, daughter of McDougall of Dunollie, in 1827.
As his older brother, John Campbell, the laird of Baleveolan, was
unmarried, Ann and Peter's son Donald, born in 1830 shortly
before Peter's death, became heir. Anne married again, but the
running of the Lismore estate was undertaken by her brother Allan
McDougall (1798–1876), in trust for her son. Although a Writer
to the Signet, like Cheyne, he had a more conventional career as
an Edinburgh lawyer. Most of the letters from 1831 to 1846 are
from McDougall to Coll Livingston (1773–1842) and then his
son Alexander (1815–1906), who acted as ground officers for the

estate, ensuring that the factor's instructions were followed. There are also letters to Rev. Gregor McGregor, asking him to make sure that the Livingstons were being firm with the tenants.

When McDougall took charge, farming had not recovered from the recession that followed the end of the Napoleonic Wars. Nearly all of the 13 or 14 tenants were in arrears of rent, and some were very seriously in trouble. From 1838 his policy was to write off arrears if the tenants would invest their own time in Improvement, particularly enclosing the land with dykes, digging ditches, and installing stone drains to supersede the time-honoured rig and furrow drainage system. Coll Livingston was charged with supervising the work and arranging a fair valuation. Rather than moving to a system of intensive grazing, as on Cheyne's land, McDougall wanted to keep his tenants but to increase the yield of their crops, and their incomes, by better husbandry. In 1839 he decreed that all of the farms must move to a Lowland-style six-course rotation in place of continuous cereals: a first cereal crop undersown with ryegrass and clover, followed by a hay crop, two years of grazing, a second cereal crop and then a green crop (turnips or potatoes). Two successive 'white' crops (oats or barley) were prohibited. In the early years the estate met the costs and carriage of grass seed and even arranged for the shipment of guano to meet the phosphate needs of the new crops, particularly turnips. When the series of letters stops in the mid-1840s, McDougall's campaign of Improvement had progressed to the planting of shelter belts, with the trees and planting overseer provided by the estate, the fencing by the tenants. They were left with little doubt that they would be severely punished if grazing stock broke into these enclosures.

Allan McDougall was, clearly, a fair and far-sighted factor. As well as ordering his tenants, through his ground officers, to Improve, he also sought to reason with them, sending pamphlets on Improved methods. There were also prizes for the best cattle on the estate. One letter to Alexander Livingston points out that if they did not raise levels of production, the repeal of the Corn Laws (removing the protection of British farmers in 1846) would lead to ruin. The response of some of the tenants was that they would rather pay their arrears than adopt the new rotation. Meeting resistance of this kind all the way, his letters are full of frustration that they did not recognise their common interest with the landowner in improving the fertility of their holdings.

What is difficult to accept is McDougall's attitude to the cottars on the estate. Weavers, labourers, shoemaker, publican and merchant, they were all due to pay rent for their houses and, when in arrears, they were obliged to provide manual labour at the Campbell Drumavuic estate. By 1840 McDougall had lost patience with the cottars and decided to evict them all, destroying their houses. Coll Livingston was offered a cash bonus for each cottar he could remove. Sense appears to have prevailed and a compromise was reached: the minister Rev. Gregor McGregor was to choose who was to remain on the estate, free of charge. McDougall was to be frustrated again as the number of people in cottar houses fell only from 44 to 41 in the decade 1841 to 1851, but many more were to go in the 1850s.

Clearance, Eviction and Emigration

In all, between the censuses of 1841 and 1861, the destruction of the communities in Kilcheran, Baligrundle and Fiart had caused a net loss of 150 people, not allowing for normal population growth or the fact that new workers were brought in from outside. Only a very few families from the three townships were able to remain on the island. However, over this 20-year period the total population of Lismore fell from 1,148 to 865, indicating that more than 135 people had left the rest of the island. There were no areas of real population growth, and there were significant net losses of population at Baleveolan (18), Balimakillichan (23), Balnagowan (12), Craignich (15), Killean (23), Laggan (13), Portcharron (23) and Sailean (10). As we shall see in the next chapter, few of these changes were associated with reductions in numbers of farmers and crofters. Instead, it seems that the poorest group, the landless cottars and labourers, moved on, possibly starved out by the potato famine. It is ironic that James Cheyne junior also decided on a new life in New Zealand in the year of his father's death.

Without similar information on the activities of other island landlords at this time, it is easy to identify James Cheyne as being responsible for the worst excesses of this period of clearance. It seems plain that he made little provision on the island for those he evicted, apart from building one or two cottages at Achnacroish. It was a harsh society that awarded Cheyne £2,000 of state aid to drain his farms but nothing for the resettlement of those who had lived there for many generations. Of the families in the three townships, only two were provided with livings: Allan Black, one of the farmers at Baligrundle, and James Black, a labourer there, were employed as shepherds at Kilcheran and Tirlaggan by 1861. Nearly 80, James was still shepherding at Fiart in 1881, but Allan had died a pauper at Kilcheran in the 1870s. Up to three other families of craftsmen and labourers seem to have found alternative accommodation at Killean, Port Ramsay and Tirlaggan.

Evidence to the Napier Commission suggests that, of the others, relatively few went to America and the colonies. It is likely that, without significant resources, most made their way by steamer to areas of potential employment in the west of Scotland. This is supported by analysis of census returns: of 324 families or individuals born on Lismore but resident elsewhere in Scotland by 1851, 127 were still within Argyll, but 171 were in Glasgow and the surrounding shires (Lanark, Dumbarton, Renfrew and Ayr). In later years there was a steady flow of young people back to the island who gave their place of birth as Glasgow, Greenock or Dumbarton in the 1861 census (Chapter 10). The heartless approach of the Cheyne family seems to be typified by the actions of his widow, Frances Charlton, who continued to live at Kilcheran for a few years after his death. Hugh Cameron (Plate 13), cottar and sailor in Killean, testified to the Napier Commission that Charlton decided that the four houses she had built in the township were too good for paupers and, instead, rented them out.

Clearly, the loss of more than a quarter of the island population, on top of earlier emigration, and the understandable instability felt by those living in townships that had not been cleared, must have been very traumatic. As we shall see in the next chapter, the islanders were right to be apprehensive.

Bibliography

Fergusson, J. (1951) *Argyll in the Forty-Five*. London: Faber & Faber.

Gray, M. (1957) *The Highland Economy, 1750–1850*. Edinburgh: Oliver & Boyd.

Hay, R.K.M. (2005) *Lochnavando No More: The Life and Death of a Moray Farming Community, 1750–1850*. Edinburgh: John Donald.

Hunter, C. (2004) *Smuggling in West Argyll and Lochaber before 1745*. Oban: Charles Hunter.

Hunter, J. (1994) *A Dance Called America*. Edinburgh: Mainstream Publishing.

Hunter, J. (2001) *Culloden and the Last Clansman*. Edinburgh: Mainstream Publishing.

Knox, J. (1975) *A Tour through the Highlands of Scotland and the Hebride Isles in 1786*. (Facsimile of the 1787 edition) Edinburgh: James Thin.

Livingstone, A., Aikman, C.W.H. and Hart, B.S. (2001) *No Quarter Given: The Muster Roll of Prince Charles Edward Stuart's Army, 1745–46*. Glasgow: Neil Wilson Publishing.

MacCulloch, J. (1824) *The Highlands and Western Islands of Scotland*. London: Longman, Hurst, Rees, Orme, Brown & Green.

McGeachy, R.A.A. (2005) *Argyll 1730–1850*. Edinburgh: John Donald.

Pennant, T. (1998) *Tour in Scotland and Voyage to the Hebrides 1772*. Edinburgh: Birlinn.

The Royal Commission of Inquiry into the Conditions of Crofters and Cotters in the Highlands and Islands (1884).

Smith, J. (1798) *General View of the Agriculture of the County of Argyll*. Edinburgh: Mundell & Sons.

Victorian Lismore

T he detailed recording of the Scottish people, which started
with the 1841 census, allows us, for the first time, to
concentrate on the lives of the tenants, cottars and craftsmen
of the island rather than the landowners and churchmen. As well
as counting the people, the seven reports between 1841 and 1901
provide information on family relationships, occupations, farming
structures, education and standards of housing, as well as the fate
of whole townships. These were decades of rapid change, with
improved communication (roads, steamers and postal services)
breaking down the isolation of the island and forcing the move
from subsistence to participation in the national and international
economy. Pressures for change were intensified by the number
of Lismore people living in the industrial centres of the west of
Scotland but still keeping contact with the island.

Population

We have seen that it is difficult to be sure of population sizes at
the start of the nineteenth century but, from 1841, the trend was
consistently downwards: 1,148 (1841), 1,010 (1851), 865 (1861),
720 (1871), 621 (1881), 561 (1891) and 500 (1901). Part of the
decline mid-century was caused by a continuation of the policy of
clearance by Cheyne's wife. In the 1860s the six farms (varying in
extent from 12 to 50 acres) and a 4-acre croft in Craignich were
completely cleared, and a single shepherd took the place of 50 to
60 people. One of the farmers, Archibald Campbell, became an

estate ground officer based at Tirlaggan, and he is remembered for his firmness in dealing with tenants. Another Campbell family took on a farm at Achinduin, but most of the other inhabitants of the township had disappeared from Lismore by 1871. On the death of Frances Charlton in 1874, the entire estate was sold to the Duke of Argyll.

However, as in earlier years, there was a continuous loss of people from elsewhere in the island throughout the century. Cloichlea was turned into a sheep run by 1871, providing a living for one family until the end of the century. The ancient township of Tirfuir, probably the original farmland of the broch, had lost all of its three or four families by 1871, although the neighbouring Balure ('New Township') had seven or eight holdings of 9 to 30 acres up to 1891. These had reduced to three by 1901. Creckanbreck, the northernmost farm of the Baleveolan estate, which supported four households in 1861, appears to have been deserted by 1881. In some areas the losses were principally landless cottars, labourers and craftsmen. Killean lost six households (the population dropped from 112 to 77 people) between 1841 and 1891 without any change in the number of farms (six), and over the same period there was a net loss of 30 people at Balnagowan but a continuation of three or four farms. Elsewhere, there was also a reduction in farming units by amalgamation (see below). In 1851 the estate of Baleveolan (including Balimakillichan) supported 132 people and 24 households on 14 land holdings (farms of 17.5 to 60 acres, and one croft of 2 acres); the community included cottars, labourers, weavers, a joiner and two merchants. As the decades passed, the population declined with the number of holdings (eight by 1861, five by 1871, four by 1891), and by the end of the century, fewer than 50 people lived on the estate.

Even though parts of the island were effectively depopulated, no real centre of population, with church, school, inn, shop and smithy, developed in the nineteenth century. None of the landlords was interested in supporting services other than those, such as the repair of implements, which affected the farming of their lands. Of the two townships with more than 100 inhabitants, Kilcheran was destroyed in the Cheyne clearances, and although Killean continued to have the greatest concentration of people (64 in 1901), with smithy, pauper houses, tradesmen and postman, it was not really a

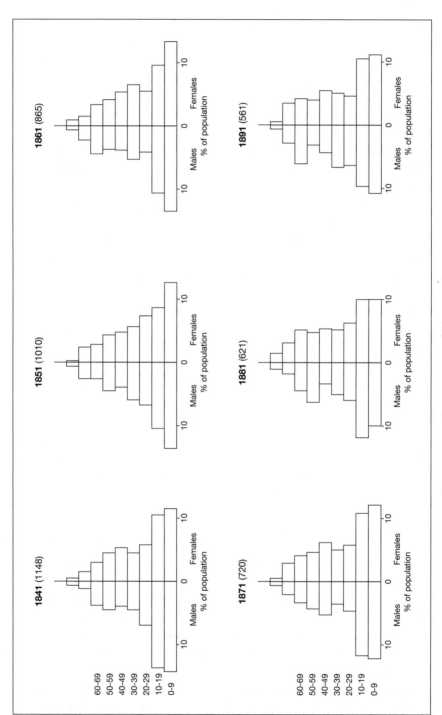

FIGURE 10.1 Age structure of Lismore 1841–91.

social or economic centre. Two other settlements, Port Ramsay (56 in 1891) and Achnacroish (growing from around ten households with the construction of the steamer pier in 1882), remained principally residential. Of the islands, Eilean nan Caoraich (Sheep Island) had one or two households occupied in the lime trade for most of the century, and two families of lightkeepers lived on Eilean Musdile.

The distribution of population by age at each census (Figure 10.1) allows us to move from considering households to individuals. An undisturbed population would show a regular 'Christmas tree' shape, with the proportion of the population declining progressively with age, owing to mortality. Even though the recording of age in 1841 was not entirely satisfactory, the distribution suggests that there had already been substantial losses of people in the intermediate age groups (20–49). However, this is shown most clearly in 1861: teenage males (10–19) had made up 10.5 per cent of the whole population in 1851 but by 1861 the same age class (now 20–29) had fallen to 4.1 per cent. This loss of two-thirds of the young men in their 20s (106 down to 36) in the 1850s, must have been a very serious blow to the morale of the island. Many are known to have gone as ploughmen to the Lowlands, but there was also a steady stream of islanders seeking a new life abroad, responding to family letters describing the hardships of their new life but also emphasising their freedom from the domination of landlords. The effects on the age structure appear as a distinct 'notch' up to the end of the century. The 1861 census shows that, similarly, the reduction in the female population was disproportionately in the 20 to 29 age group (decline from 87 to 46), and the trend for younger people to leave the island continued in the 1860s (1871 census).

Figure 10.1 reveals several other features of the Lismore population. Up to 1871, children under ten made up around a quarter of the people on the island, but there were many more surviving boys than girls. This was most obvious in 1841, when there were 162 boys to 131 girls, but the pattern continued until 1881. Although, as elsewhere, male mortality was greater, the higher numbers of male children meant that women did not predominate in the older age classes. In 1791 Rev. Donald McNicol reported on the unusual longevity of the people of his parish, referring to the many men and women over 80, not to mention the few who reached 100, but the census data for the nineteenth century does not support the idea of great longevity on Lismore: only about 1 in 20 of the population were over 70 and a total of three men and one woman reached 90 over the period.

The People

Out of the 96 'fencible men' on the island in 1692, not long after the Scottish (as opposed to the Gaelic) method of adopting family names had become normal, exactly half were Blacks (written as McIllguich), Carmichaels, McIntyres, Campbells or McColls. There was only one McCorquodale and no McGregors, but several McCicks, McKellaichs, McLauchlanes, McOanleys and Stewarts. By 1841 one out of every five families (21 per cent) was called Black or McColl, and nearly three-quarters of the people (70 per cent) had one of seven surnames (Black, McColl, Carmichael, McIntyre, McCorquodale, McGregor and Campbell). There were at least five families each of Buchanans, Livingstones, McDonalds, McLachlans and Kieths.

These names can be divided into a few main groups. First, there are three which appear to originate in the Christian past of the island: Black (variously McIlleDhuibh, McIllguich, and interpreted as son of the servant of the Lismore abbot 'An Dubhach'); Carmichael (anglicisation of McGillemichael, son of the servant of St Michael, the popular saint of the West Highlands); and Livingstone, which we have seen derives from McLeay or McOanley. Next in importance are common names of Lorn and Lochaber, which probably date back to the MacDonald lordship of the Isles (McColl closely associated with the Stewarts of Appin; McIntyre originally based in Glencoe; McLachlan). In the nineteenth century at least, McKellaich seems to have been used interchangeably with McDonald. Names from further afield in Argyll include the various forms of McEachern originating in Kintyre (McCick, McCaig, McKeich, anglicised to Kieth – not to be confused with Keith, although the latter spelling became universal) and the Norse/Gaelic McCorquodale from Loch Awe. The two name lists indicate that the Blacks, Carmichaels, McCaigs, Kieths, Livingstones, McColls, McDonalds and McLachlans have a very long history on the island, whereas the Buchanans (from Loch Lomond) McCorquodales and McGregors probably arrived in the service of the Campbell landlords.

There was also a restricted range of Christian names. In 1841 nearly three-quarters (70 per cent) of males had been baptised John, Donald, Duncan, Dugald, Archibald or Hugh. Of these, four are traditional Gaelic names (Hugh being the anglicisation of Aodh or Eoghan), John was a popular saint, and the Germanic personal name Archibald (translated as Gilleasbeag, bishop's son) was particularly common in Clan Campbell. In larger families the list extended to Alexander, James, Neil and Malcolm. Following the pattern elsewhere in Scotland, seven out of ten women had one of three saints' names: Mary, Catherine (including Kate variations) or Anne. The next most popular names were Peggy (including a few Margarets), Janet, Isabella (Bella), Kirsty/Chirsty and Jean/Jane.

This shows that, before the Victorian era, there was only limited intrusion of people from elsewhere – only 34 out of the 1,148 residents in 1841 had not been born on the island. This continued throughout the century, with only 14 per cent of the 1891 residents being incomers but, towards the end, with the population falling to 500, the proportion of immigrants rose to nearly a quarter (23.2 per cent in 1901). The incomers fell into four main categories: immigrants from the immediate surroundings (Appin, Benderloch, Ardchattan, Oban, Kingairloch, Morvern and Mull) as wives, skilled workers or servants; the children of emigrants, returning mainly from Glasgow, Greenock and Dumbarton (see below); and shepherds and farmers brought in by Improving landlords from the south-west of Scotland (Dumfries and Galloway) and the sheep-rearing areas of the West Highlands. The thriving coastal trade in lime and coal brought boat owners and sailors from the west coast (Tiree, Kintyre and Wester Ross) and, in the last decade, several families arrived from South Uist, Morvern and Mull. This preponderance of immigration from the West Highlands and Islands and from emigrant communities ensured that, at the turn of the century, virtually all of the people living on the island spoke Gaelic. A majority were bilingual in Gaelic and English.

To outsiders, the Lismore people had developed particular characteristics. In 1841 Rev. Gregor McGregor wrote:

There are 1430 people in Lismore, and these are so closely connected by blood relationship and intermarriage, that they are all near relations to one another. A Lismore man seldom takes a wife from any other place; but, although, as a body, they are relations and friendly to one another, yet there is a remnant of ancient feudalism still lingering among them. Every sept or clan stands by itself, to support one another against any other sept or clan that may wish to encounter them; but although they sometimes in this way quarrel at home, yet when abroad at markets they are very faithful to one another, and woe betide the unfortunate stranger who may attempt to insult the least of them.

Forty years later, under some pressure from the witnesses at the meeting with the Napier Commissioners in 1883, factor John Fraser Sim gave a similar opinion:

I wish to mention the fact that the people of Lismore are a people by themselves. On Mr Fell's property I draw rents from fifty-nine people and of these fifty-seven have been born and bred on the island. I should like to mention that fact, because it explains a peculiarity in Lismore which I think hardly finds another example in any portion of the Highlands. If you take the Balliveolan property, where there are twelve tenants, only one of these has been introduced as a stranger. All the rest are aborigines of the place; and this explains to a great extent what we have heard today of the long tenure the people have had of the land, notwithstanding the fact that there are practically no leases in the island, with the exception of those of the larger holdings. They have their own habits, customs, and sympathies; they are clannish when they get amongst strangers; they fight a good deal amongst themselves; they have their own patron saint; and altogether the island is an island by itself.

Families

With the experience of the extreme hardships of the 1840s, the loss of so many young people in the 1850s, and the steady reduction in opportunities to earn their living on the island, those who remained on the island were less inclined to marry. In 1851 (the first census to include marital status), umarried adults over the age of 25 made up 13 per cent of the total island population, but the level rose with time, reaching nearly one out of five (18 per cent) in 1891 and 1901. The heads of many households were unmarried and brothers and sisters tended to remain together to conserve the family resources.

The same economic and demographic pressures meant that men tended to delay marrying until their 30s, when they were more able to support a family. Estimates from 47 families in 1851 and 23 families in 1891 show that the average age at marriage remained at 33 or 34, compared with 26 or 27 for women. Even for women early marriage was unusual. In 1851 only one girl had married before the age of 20, and several were well into their 30s before having their first child. The resulting reduction in the number of childbearing years was another factor in the decline in the island population. Nevertheless, families of five or more living children were common, as were children born to mothers of over 40.

Later marriage for men meant that there were many widows. In 1851, out of 79 inhabitants who had lost their marriage partner, 62 were widows, and throughout the century there were twice as many widows as widowers. This had a major effect on family poverty, particularly since men tended to continue working to support their family into old age and it was common for widows to be evicted from their homes on the death of their husband. Before the passing of the Scottish Poor Law in 1845, the support for paupers varied widely among parishes. The legal requirement for landlords (heritors), ministers and elders of each parish to draw up a list of all their poor and to provide financial support, half provided by the heritors and half by the residents, was vague and left too much judgement in the hands of those who were called upon to pay.

The unsatisfactory situation on Lismore was described by Rev. Gregor McGregor in 1841:

> The poor … are upon the whole pretty well supported. The people are very attentive to their wants, and give them both food and raiment where most wanted: a duty which is indispensable, as the pittance which they receive in money, being not more than about 10/6 for each person yearly, would go but a short way to maintain them. The sum arises from collections at the church doors; from donations given by some of the heretors at the time of dividing the poor's money; from benefactions of a few benevolent people deceased, and from mort cloth dues, and other dues levied in the parish …

and it is interesting to note that only five people, all of them born in Ireland, were recognised as paupers in the 1841 census. With the establishment of the right to support under the act, and as a result of the evictions and hunger of the 1840s, the number of households on Lismore headed by a pauper in the census records rose sharply to 31 in 1851 and 1861, falling to 15 in 1871, three in 1881 and nine in 1891. The official Poor Law figures suggest that there were even more, for example 42 with 12 dependents in 1869. These were mainly family units where the head was a widow over 70 or a widow with young children and, although there were paupers in several townships, they tended to concentrate in Portcharron, Killean, Baligarve and Balure. Support, normally in the form of money or clothes, supplemented by funds from bequests (particularly the Carmichael and Keith Bequests on Lismore), was generally provided to paupers living at home, although there were a few boarders with other families, and a minority were transferred to the poorhouse in Oban.

The struggle to make ends meet can be sensed from one household in Killean in 1851 made up of Effy McIntyre, an 80-year-old unmarried pauper, and her 48-year-old unmarried niece, Cathrine McColl, whose occupation was 'gathering shellfish'.

Letters written to the parish board show that some of the poor were in a miserable condition:

> Killean, Lismore
> 13 October 1869
>
> To the Chairman and members of the Parish Board of Lismore and Appin
>
> Gentlemen
> I humbly beg lieve to inform you that I am very ill for want of a pair of shoes and my feet are constantly wet and I feel it to be very harmful to my health as I am much troubled with the rheumatism pains so I trust that your Honourable Board may think proper to grant me a pair of shoes as the cold weather are now approaching.
>
> I am, gentlemen, one of your paupers
>
> John A. Carmichael

The parish board also provided medicines to the poor who were sick. In 1862 they provided 'cordials' for bronchitis and asthma, laxatives for 'gastric fever', and 'astringents' for pain. Robert McCaig, a 13-year-old herder suffering from a 'disease of the brain' seemed to be responding to 'blister purgatives'. The recording of disability and chronic illness in the census was very patchy, but several individuals described in the census records as mentally ill (for example 'imbecile from birth'), blind or deaf were being cared for within the family and not classed as paupers.

A striking feature of the 1861 census was the presence of 18 children of emigrants in the households of grandparents or uncles and aunts. They had mainly been born in Glasgow, Greenock or Dumbarton, and it appears that they had been sent 'home' to the island by parents who recognised that both their health and schooling would benefit. Some may have been illegitimate. This continued, to a lesser degree, until 1891 when there were nine children placed with relations but, over 30 years, few of these children stayed on as adults on the island.

The Carmichaels, farming at Achuran, show the Lismore extended family at work. In 1841, Donald, aged 30, was the unmarried tenant of 25 acres, supporting his widowed mother and two other unmarried brothers, Dugald, 24, and Alexander, 20. By 1851 the household had expanded to include two sisters, one married, and three nieces who had been born in Glasgow. They were resident and not visitors. Ten years later, Donald, aged 50 and still unmarried, had succeeded in increasing his acreage to 100, but he was now responsible for his 74-year-old mother; the unmarried Dugald and Alexander (designated ploughman); Donald McColl, farm labourer, 18; dairymaid Mary Kieth, 39, unmarried; and another 12-year-old niece, at school on the island. In his last appearance in 1871, Donald was at the head of an entirely unmarried household: Dugald, Alexander, Mary Kieth and John Carmichael (not related, 18, labourer). At Donald's death, the farm appears to have been split between Alexander and Dugald, and both immediately married. Aged 63 in 1881, it was too late for Dugald and his wife to have children, but Alexander (55) and Ann (33) went on to have two sons and a daughter. In 1901, Alexander, recorded as 81 years of age, was farming at Park, assisted by his unmarried sons Donald (25) and Duncan (18).

Farming

Until the early nineteenth century, visitors remarked on the predominance of cereal growing on Lismore but, with improved transport and distribution, the importance of the island as a local source of oats and barley for the production of human food and alcohol declined. Over the century, there was a progressive movement towards livestock farming and, although the productive pasture of Lismore yielded high-quality stock, the island farmers were now competing in the same market as their neighbours on the mainland, who had lower transport costs. This move away from arable farming had a major influence on the island economy and landscape.

In line with developments elsewhere in Argyll, it is likely that runrig (Chapter 7) was disappearing by 1800. Each farm was a consolidated holding but, since the technology for subsoil drainage was not generally available in Scotland until around 1830, and it was not until the 1840s that the Cheyne and Baleveolan estates were actively involved, it must have been several decades before the practice of draining by rig and furrow was finally abandoned. Before the end of the century, with the spread of stone or tile drains in the areas of heavier soil, these redundant structures were ploughed out, resulting in the flat fields of today. Where they can still be seen on the island, for example on south- and east-facing slopes at Portcharron (Plate 2) and Point, they are generally on steeper ground, unsuited to intensive agriculture. These may well be areas that were cultivated by hand during the period of very high population density and land hunger. This is almost certainly the case for the well-defined rigs on the bank behind the cottages at Port Ramsay. The change in the appearance of the island was most obvious in autumn and winter when a smoother green landscape replaced the brown corrugated stubble fields.

Excluding the areas converted by Cheyne into extensive sheep runs, the typical farm in 1851 had between 20 and 30 acres. There were only four over 50 acres and holdings of as little as 7 acres were classed as farms. Farm sizes still reflected old subdivisions. For example, there were two pairs of exactly matching farms at Baleveolan (seven holdings of 15, 17.5 (2), 20 (2), 30 and 59 acres). Many factors combined to drive the amalgamation of these small farms into larger holdings. Amongst landlords there was enthusiasm for improvement (intensification of production using more expensive inputs: improved varieties of crops, including grasses and clovers, and livestock breeds; new crops such as turnips; liming; raising the phosphate status with bone dust or guano; draining; fencing and walling; improved ploughs and other implements), with the promise of higher productivity and higher rents. The costs of many of these inputs could be reduced if spread over a greater area. On the other hand, as they moved further from a subsistence economy, the islanders needed a higher income from their farming to meet the cost of imported food, clothing and other necessities. For example, evidence given to the Napier Commissioners shows that, with the final failure of the island peat banks, expenditure on coal was a critical factor in rural poverty. The pace of change was slow in the 1850s but by 1871 the number of farmers had fallen sharply (from eight to two at Balimakillichan; from eight to three at Achinduin; from three to one at Frackersaig). By 1901 there were only 23 farmers on the island, compared with 90 in 1851, and there were several farms of between 50 and 100 acres. It is ironic that four of the holdings in 1891 were farms that had been re-established in cleared areas by the Duke of Argyll at Fiart (Fiart and Dalnarrow), Craignich and Baligrundle, although three of the farmers had been brought in from elsewhere.

Farming had changed from growing crops for rent and home consumption to a system where most of the land was devoted to supporting livestock. The principal products, Highland cattle, were sold in October at Oban at three years old and were a long way from the small beasts driven south to the markets of Falkirk and Crieff in the past, but they were normally finished for the butcher by a period of intensive feeding on the mainland. It would be well into the twentieth century before government schemes for the introduction of elite bulls, such as Shorthorns, caused a major increase in the size of island cattle. Some farms specialised in dairying, still using Highland cattle, producing butter and cheese for market; towards the end of the century these enterprises became more profitable with the arrival of more productive Dairy Shorthorn and Ayrshire cows. Where the holding included areas of rough pasture, these were exploited using the same Blackface sheep, or crosses with the Border Leicester, which dominated the cleared south-east of the island. Much of the ploughed land, which constituted 50 per cent or less of each holding in 1871 and 1881, was devoted to oats, turnips and hay for livestock feeding, including oats for the working horses and potatoes for local consumption and sale. The non-arable land was permanent pasture of varying quality.

At the same time, the workforce was evolving, and specialists emerging. By 1861, 31 men were identified specifically as ploughmen, as distinct from ordinary farm labourers, and at Park, Achuran, the Manse, Killandrist, Sailean, Frackersaig, Tirlaggan and Achnacroish there was enough work to justify employing a dairymaid. In 1891 there was a shepherd at Craignich, Sailean, Baleveolan, Frackersaig and Achinduin, and two at Kilcheran. Although there are no records of the progress of enclosure, in 1841 there were 16 herds, mostly teenage boys and girls, but by 1891 there was work for only two boys to keep the cows out of the corn. The Lismore Agricultural Society, founded in 1853, contributed to the improvement of skills and the introduction of new ideas in farming by organising annual ploughing matches and agricultural shows.

Crofting

Lismore crofts, commonly of as little as 2 or 3 acres arable with associated common grazing, had developed in different ways. Across the island, the subdivision of townships to provide cottars with smallholdings to supplement their income from providing farm labour had, in a few cases, resulted in the recognition of small units of land, let separately from the other farms in the township. This seems to have been the case for the single crofts, in the first half of the century, at Achuran, Balimakillichan, Balure and Craignich. These disappeared in the process of farm amalgamation. The ten crofts and small farms at Killean, rented at between £7 and £10 per annum, had evolved out of the need for members of the community of tradesmen (see below) to have a potato patch and grazing for the family cow.

As explained in Chapter 9, the crofts at Port Ramsay and, possibly, Laggan had been established to secure a workforce for the Duke of

Argyll's plan to exploit the herring fisheries. The 16 lots (3.5 acres each with the right to graze one cow on the 65 acres of common grazing) at Port Ramsay were not intended to provide a living in themselves. Indeed, evidence presented to the Napier Commission indicated that the common grazing was quite inadequate for their needs. The community struggled to make its living until the lime trade took off in the 1850s and by 1861 it included two shipowners, two captains, five sailors, two ship carpenters/boat builders and a quarryman. Only four of the inhabitants classed themselves solely as crofters, and none did in 1871.

In response to serious unrest in crofting areas of Wester Ross, Lewis and Skye, and the precedent set by land reform in Ireland, the government set up a team of commissioners under Lord Napier to investigate the underlying grievances across the Highlands and Islands and the Northern Isles. The commissioners duly arrived on Lismore on 13 August 1883 and convened in the Baptist chapel at Bachuil to hear evidence from ten farmers and crofters chosen as representatives at earlier meetings, the teacher at Baligarve public school, and the factor for the Fell and Baleveolan estates. From the outset, it was clear that the level of rents was not a major issue, although the rising cost of living, particularly coal, was causing problems. Concern was expressed about security of tenure without written leases (and the related eviction of widows even though they had sons who could take on the holding), but the strongest criticism was of the landlords' policy on the improvement and maintenance of property. Formerly, the farmer or crofter would build his own house and steading but the trend by the 1880s, with rising standards of housing, was for the cost to be shared with the landlord. However, interest on any investment by the landlord had to be paid annually by the tenant at between 6.5 and 7.5 per cent. This was effectively a rise in rent, and it hardly encouraged improvements in living and working conditions (see below). Even more seriously, factors valued each property regularly and, if a tenant left or was evicted, he would be expected to compensate the landlord for any depreciation. Instead of compensation for the money *he* had invested in his house and steading, the outgoing tenant was penalised for any deterioration.

The commissioners worked quickly to digest the enormous amount of information they had amassed and, in 1886, the Crofters'

Holdings Act (Scotland) was passed. Taking the threshold for a croft to be a rental value (£30 per annum rather than an area), the act ensured security of tenure and a guarantee that the tenancy would pass to the next generation; a formal process for appeal against unfair rents; and compensation for improvements on the croft. It dealt with the main grievances of the Lismore crofters and, by the 1891 census, other small farming units at Achnacroish, Achinduin, Baleveolan, Balnagowan (two), Balure (three) and Tirlaggan were recognised as crofts. More were to follow in later years.

Occupations

Other than the farmers and crofters, most of the people of the island were generalists, turning their hand to the work available at home or elsewhere. Men described as labourers, farm or general servants, could, at different times of the year, be employed in farm work, at the lime kilns, bringing in peat from the mainland or mending roads. Women were described as general or domestic servants, even though most of them were working at home. As there were few 'big houses', most of the women who went into service had to leave Lismore. The island also needed a range of skilled craftsmen and tradesmen.

With the reduction in grain growing, there was less demand for the work of millers. Of the many water-powered mills built by Lismore landlords, only two corn mills, between Baligrundle and Kilcheran, and at Balnagowan, were still in operation in 1841, and with the clearance of the south-east quarter of the island, the Balnagowan mill operated alone from 1860 onwards. Its mill lade and wheel have survived to the present day, although the mill building is in ruins. Mill remains can also be seen at Miller's Port. Up to the middle of the century, there was a resident wright whose job it was to maintain heavy wooden machinery, such as the mill workings, and build and repair carts. As we shall see in the next section, although his job had disappeared by 1871, there were many other craftsmen in wood throughout the century.

There was plenty of work for the two smithies at Killean and Clachan/ Baligarve (the latter recently converted into a dwelling-houses), as farming became more mechanised and the demand increased for domestic appliances and tools. By 1881 there were four blacksmiths, with John Black setting up as a specialist 'engine smith' at Achnacroish. Most of the Lismore smiths were incomers. Dugald McPherson, originally from Oban, served the island from Clachan for more than 30 years from the 1870s and was joined in 1901 by his son Hector, who continued the family tradition for half a century.

There were also opportunities for stonemasons. Their number increased from one only (the Malcom McColl in Tirlaggan who was imprisoned after the 1843 deforcement) to six in 1891, and they were all Lismore-born. In the early decades of the century most people were living in a form of 'blackhouse', constructed by themselves of dry stone, with a thatched roof, a central hearth and no windows. The internal walls of ruined cottages at Sailean show good examples of the slots which carried the timber roof supports down nearly to ground level. The transition to improved standards took a long time. Ruined townships such as Portcharron, not abandoned until late in the century, have a mixture of dwelling-houses, only some of which have mortared walls and gable chimneys, but the census shows that all of the houses there had at least one room with a window. The transition is very clear at Creckanbreck, which was occupied up to the 1880s. Three of the dwelling houses are of dry-stone construction, with the internal walls sealed with clay plastering, and they lack gable hearths and chimneys. The double cottage shows signs of later mortaring. Lower down the slope lies a more recent house with durable lime mortaring and a monumental limestone mantel over the hearth in the south gable.

The improvement in the housing stock is most evident for farmhouses. By 1861 most had at least three rooms and, by 1891 Baligrundle, Balnagowan, Clachan, Craignich, Dalnarrow, Frackersaig, Kilcheran, Park and Point Farm Houses had five or more. The same period saw the building of new schools and manses (see below), as well as large private houses built of dressed stone with slated roofs (Bachuil House and Hawthorn House, each with 11 rooms; Daisybank at Baleveolan, with nine rooms, occupied by 1901). The Parish Manse, built originally in 1749, was expanded to 19 rooms. Nevertheless, at the start of the twentieth century many of the families of cottars, labourers and paupers were living crowded into one room. James Wilson, teacher at the public school at Baligarve, told the Napier Commissioners in 1883 that, for crofters

> the house accommodation ... is very bad, the houses being all thatch, and the wood-work, and such, of a very rude sort. Hardly any of the doors have locks, but, in place, any rude contrivance that the people may invent; and with a north west gale their places are made very uncomfortable. There is also very little accommodation for the stock.

but he did confirm that the houses had chimneys.

The census records show the effects of the early globalisation of the textile industries. Jane Drummond (55) in Balnagowan in 1841 was the last recorded spinster (as an occupation) on the island and, although there were handloom weavers producing woollen cloth at Baleveolan, Balimakillichan, Kilcheran, Killean, Portcharron and Port Ramsay up to 1851, John McDougall in Balimakillichan kept up his lonely role as the last Lismore weaver until 1881, when he was 77. However, the increasing availability of cheap textiles provided work for between three and five tailors until the end of the century. In 1901 Neil McCormick, resident at his new villa (Daisybank), and describing himself as 'Taylor, clothier, grocer & general merchant', provided employment for three assistants, making uniforms for steamers and private yachts. From 1861 onwards there was always at least one dressmaker and, in 1871 Mary Black had set herself up as a shirtmaker in Balimakillichan to support her pauper mother. For most of the century, there were three to five shoemakers/cobblers, distributed across the island, whose work was probably more repair than making as industrially-produced shoes became more available.

Many factors combined to increase the demand for imported food and drink: these included the trend away from grain production, improvements in transport and communication (not least the regular steamer services), and a developing taste for luxury items, particularly tea. The role of 'grocer and general merchant' to the island was dominated by the Stewart family for much of the century. Mary Stewart (62) was established in business at Baleveolan in 1841 and she had been succeeded by her son John by 1861. He was a joiner to trade, but prospered as merchant at Bachuil until the end of the century, when he was able to retire in comfort to Hawthorn House. At different times there were also general merchants at Tirlaggan (1841, 1861, 1881), Kilcheran (1851), Achnacroish (1861), Stronacroibh (1871), Portcharron (1871), Sailean (1881, 1891) and Achuran (1891).

Lismore had a long reputation for distilling and consuming alcohol. In 1791 there were seven or eight inns and, in 1841 Rev. Gregor McGregor was exercised about the many dram shops in the parish. However, as the century progressed, the number of licensed premises generally declined, perhaps under pressure from the church. In 1841, unlike earlier years, there was no hospitality associated with the island ferry crossings, and the only public houses were at Kilcheran and Baleveolan. Within ten years, Donald McColl had started his business as 'vintner' in Taynlochan, moving in the 1850s to set up an inn at Point, providing courage for travellers crossing to Port Appin. Archibald Campbell provided the same service at Achnacroish and both continued until after 1871, when McColl reached 90 years of age. By 1881 there were no public houses on Lismore and the inn at Point had been converted into a temperance hotel.

The Island Specialists: Boat Builders, Lime Burners and Sea Captains

For an island lacking any standing timber, Lismore had an astonishing number of craftsmen in wood – between 12 and 15 in the period 1841–61, eventually dwindling to less than five by the turn of the century. The explanation lies in a strong tradition of boat building by three or four dynasties of ship carpenters. Niel McDonald and his two sons, Duncan and Donald, who worked from Kilcheran, building small boats for inshore fishing and harvesting seaweed (Plate 15), lost their living in the Cheyne clearances. Duncan's evidence to the Napier Commissioners in 1883 provides a unique insight into Cheyne's tactics during the clearance of the south-east of the island (see pages 135–138). Settling in Port Ramsay, he was still working in 1881, at the age of 70, with his stepson, but before 1891 the business had transferred to Oban. Two clamps, hand-made by the McDonalds, used in the construction of clinker-built boats, can be seen in the Lismore Museum.

Two generations of the Connel family operated as boat builders and carpenters out of Balure throughout the century. Their sawpit is in a cleft of rock near the shore at Baileouchdarach, and one of their long crosscut saws could still be found there in recent times. Another sawpit was close to Balure steading. Although no direct link can be established, it is almost certain that these Connels were the descendants of the Clann Mhic Gille Chonaill, hereditary shipwrights to the Campbells of Glenorchy (Chapter 7). In 1841 Rev. Donald McNicol described another boat-building workshop in the great sea cave at Sailean and, although no traces of this activity remain inside the cave, there is a clearly recognisable sawpit on the seaward side (Plate 14a). The carpenter, Donald McIntyre, must have had considerable difficulty in bringing in his timber and launching his boats down a very rocky shore. By 1861 he is described as a master ship-carpenter at Achnacroish, employing two, including an apprentice.

At Balure, throughout the Victorian era, there were also families of joiners, McCallums and Blacks, who must have cooperated with the boat builders, particularly in the import of supplies of timber. In 1851 Anne Connel (14) had moved into the McCallum household to assist their widowed mother, indicating that there was a functional relationship between the different woodworking families. The fact that the Balure joiners described themselves as wright and cartwright in the 1861 census shows that they did not restrict themselves to house fitting. At different times, there were also single-handed joiners at Achnacroish, Achinduin, Achuran, Baleveolan, Balnagowan, Portcharron and Tirlaggan, responding to the demands for improved housing.

The 15 or 16 lime kilns at six sites on Lismore and Eilean nan Caoraich, described in great detail in a recent report commissioned by Historic Scotland, testify to a major Victorian industry. The first large-scale kiln was built at Kilcheran around 1804 and the complex of three kilns there operated until around 1840. Lime burning at Sailean (Plate 14b, 15) and Park had been established by 1825–30, probably earlier at Sailean, but the origin and duration of the activities at Alisrath, Port na Morlach and Eilean nan Caoraich are less clear. All three sites probably started around 1850. Lismore was the main supplier of lime to the West Highlands and Islands for building and agriculture. For example, in 1847 Lord Salisbury

sent the steamer *Ramsgate Packet* to Lismore for 200 barrels of
lime for the improvements to Kinloch House on Rum. In 1878 the
combined output of Sailean, Park and Eilean nan Caoraich was
estimated to be the equivalent of 48,000 barrels of slaked lime,
but the completion of the Callander and Oban Railway in 1880,
bringing cheap bulk supplies, undermined the profitability of the
industry. Lime could be made much more economically in areas
of Carboniferous rocks in the Midland Valley of Scotland and in
northern England, where limestone and coal occurred together.
The smaller kilns went out of business, leaving Park and Eilean
nan Caoraich to continue up to the eve of the First World War.
Sailean, where the last lime was burnt in 1934, was by far the
most successful business, resulting in a complex industrial site with
coal and explosive stores, office and residential accommodation,
an impressive quay, and a huge scar in the cliff where limestone
was quarried for 100 years (Plate 14b).

The lime industry, owned by the landlords, was leased to small-
scale entrepreneurs, who organised coal supplies, quarrying,
burning, packing and transport. In the second half of the century,
two generations of the McIntyre family were in charge of the
Sailean enterprise, including the supply of coal to householders.
In the evidence to the Napier Commission, they are singled out
as the major (and unusually enlightened) employers on the island,
providing a livelihood for families cleared from the land. The lease
for Park Farm included operation of the limekilns, which, at times,
was sublet with the agreement of the landlord. In her evidence to
the Napier Commissioners, Mary Carmichael, the widow evicted
from Park, described the difficulties of handling this subletting
(presumably to Donald Black, the 'lime burner' at Port Ramsay).
The joint activity of farming and lime burning, involving a great
deal of transporting by cart, explains the high quality of the stables
and cartshed on the farm, built around 1840.

The census records are not helpful in revealing the extent of
employment in the lime industry, probably because many men
working at the quarries and kilns will have described themselves
simply as 'labourer'. In 1881, at the height of the industry, there
were four 'quarriers' living near the Park kiln (Point, Port Ramsay
and Laggan) but the three 'lime workers' (Balnagowan and
Baligarve), the 'quarry labourer' (Tirlaggan) and the 'limestone

miner' (Achnacroish) had a long way to walk to work at Sailean. Their employer, Duncan McIntyre (limestone quarrier and farmer), was based at Tirlaggan. It is also difficult to identify the associated workers. For example, only in 1871 is there any mention of a cooper (Donald Black in Baleveolan, brother-in-law of one of the lime burners). On Eilean nan Caoraich, all the work was done by two resident families who looked to Port Appin for their support and supplies.

The wages paid to the teams of quarry workers, possibly 20 to 30 men in total, were only part of the prosperity brought to the island by the lime industry. By 1861 at least four sailing smacks were based at Port Ramsay, bringing coal from Lanarkshire for the Sailean and Park kilns, and carrying the very hazardous quicklime around the west coast. These fast little ships, the forerunners of the Puffers, were single-masted sloops or cutters, gaff-rigged with long bowsprits. The largest smacks operating in Scottish waters were up to 66 feet in length and 18 feet in breadth, carrying 70 tons of cargo but, with a draught of only 6 feet, they had access to island quays and jetties. Early photographs (Plate 15) show smacks of different sizes tied up at the quay at Sailean but, since the anchorage there is limited and exposed, Port Ramsay became a bustling harbour, with the cottages occupied by interlinked seafaring families of McCorquodales, Carmichaels and McDonalds. In 1881 they were joined by McFadyen and McKinnon sea captains from Tiree.

For long an island preoccupied by the land, Lismore was turning to the sea for its living. There is no doubt that, with the many small boats built on the island and the abundance of fish, the people had traditionally supplemented their diet from the sea. In 1841 Rev. Gregor McGregor recorded that herring were very plentiful at times, particularly in Airds Bay, and that the people of his parish secured 'considerable quantities' as well as 'cuddies, both large and small, in vast shoals; red or rock cod, lythes, mackerel, and a few flounders'. However, in that year, only four men were described as sailor, seaman or mariner and none as full-time fisherman. By 1871, across the island there were 11 sailors, 6 shipowners or masters, 11 fishermen, 1 boatman and 1 ferryman, all but three of whom were born on the island. The Lismore graveyard testifies to the increased frequency of drowning from the middle of the century.

Communications

During the eighteenth century and for much of the Victorian era, the development and maintenance of the country's infrastructure was the responsibility of committees of local landlords who, as justices of the peace and commissioners of supply, generated much of the investment by taxation of property holders (in terms of money and labour) and charges for the use of roads and ferries. Until road travel on the mainland improved, Lismore was seen as a highway to Mull, for example for soldiers based on the garrison established at Duart after the '45, using the short sea crossings at each end of the island. In 1752 the local commissioners met to deal with complaints about the lack of a ferry from Fiart to Mull. To finance the service, they proposed a charge of 6d per person and 10d per horse.

In 1832 their successors, the Lorn District Road Trustees, reviewed the three ferry services affecting Lismore. For the crossing from Port Appin, there were two (open) boats and two ferrymen (one living at Point in 1841) and the charge per person was 6d each way. Cows cost 6d, but carrying horses was clearly hazardous: 9d each, rising to 1s 5d if the horse was shod and likely to damage the boat. At the north end there was also the possibility, on request, of an expensive passage across Loch Linnhe to Kingairloch (4s 6d from Appin, 3s 6d from Lismore). In spite of the lack of a sheltered port at the south end, there was still a Fiart–Mull ferry (2s 6d per person, horse or cow). By 1851 traffic to Mull had fallen away and the Point of Fiart boatman was engaged to support the Musdile lighthouse. Although tenants on Lismore were required to provide two or three day's labour each year on the island roads, they remained well below the standards being achieved on the mainland in the 1840s, and this continued for the rest of the century.

It is difficult to overestimate the impact on island communities such as Lismore of the west coast steamers, pioneered by the *Comet* from 1819, long before the arrival of railways. By 1841 steamers connecting Glasgow, Mull, Fort William and Skye called at Lismore twice a week in summer and once in winter. After the construction of the Achnacroish pier by the Duke of Argyll in 1882, the *Iona* called each day on its way between Oban and

Fort William. Manufactured items were delivered quickly, with perishable eggs and dairy products going in the opposite direction, and contact could be maintained between the island and its many emigrants in the south. However, the most important improvement was in the postal service, which was far from satisfactory until the establishment of a full Post Office at Achnacroish in the 1880s under the supervision of John Shankland, who combined the roles of piermaster, postmaster and farmer. Earlier, the nearest Post Office had been at Port Appin, and deliveries to the island were made twice a week to a 'sub-Post Office' at Portcharron (later Clachan), from which they were distributed through the island by a 'postrunner' or 'letter carrier'. The daily arrival of the *Iona* extended to the people of Lismore the standards of postal communication enjoyed by the rest of Victorian Britain.

Church and School

Of the three Presbyterian churches that emerged out of the realignments of the 1840s, the Established Church of Scotland initially retained most of its members on Lismore, presumably under pressure from the Duke of Argyll and other landlords who did not wish to lose control of church appointments. Gregor McGregor, the minister in place at the time of the Disruption in 1843, remained a stalwart of the Established Church (joined by only one other minister in the presbytery), and continued up to the age of 88 in 1885. The detached part of the parish in Kingairloch was served by a church missionary, based in Morvern, who ministered on alternate Sundays at the appointed preaching station in the public house at Kingairloch. In 1836 the Presbytery of Lorn reported that only between six and ten people crossed Loch Linnhe regularly to attend church on Lismore.

Meanwhile, the United Presbyterian Church, in the person of Rev. William Wood, mounted a major evangelical campaign on the island. Optimistically, in the late 1840s, the new congregation built a church for 250 at Baligrundle, although it rarely housed more than 100. The third branch, the Free Church of Scotland, attracted fewer members in Lismore and Appin parish and, before the formal union in 1900, they joined the United Presbyterians at Baligrundle to form what would be the United Free Church. These were not the only possibilities for Protestant worship on the island as Alexander Livingston, the Baron of Bachuil, became a Baptist minister and missionary, setting up a chapel at Bachuil in the 1860s; a small group of Congregationalists maintained another chapel from the 1880s; and there were other independent preachers and tract distributors.

In the decades before the 1872 Education Act, which made attendance at school obligatory between the ages of 5 and 14, elementary schooling on the island was provided at different times at parish schools at Achuran, Baligarve, Baligrundle and Killandrist. The leading schoolmaster of the age was Samuel McColl, originally from Appin, who served as session clerk and parochial schoolmaster at Killandrist from 1809 to 1862. At the transition to the new state-controlled system, schooling transferred to schools built at Baligarve and Baligrundle.

Before compulsory schooling, Lismore already had an excellent record. In the 1850s and 1860s, three-quarters of all boys and girls aged 5 to 10 were scholars and, between 1851 and 1861, the attendance for teenagers up to 15 rose from 54 per cent to 74 per cent. Those out of school and in paid employment, mainly as servants and herders, fell from one in four to one in ten. Five or six pupils remained in school on the island over the age of 15 and up to 18.

Eminent Victorians

From their sound educational grounding at parish schools on Lismore, two national figures emerged, one of whom died before the reign of Victoria but influenced later scientific thinkers. Dugald Carmichael (1772–1827) was born at Stronacroibh and educated at Achuran Parish School, gaining the opportunity to study arts and medicine at Glasgow and Edinburgh Universities. By signing up as an army surgeon, he was able to make pioneering botanical collections in South Africa, Mauritius, India and the isolated island of Tristan da Cunha, where he is said to have made the first ascent of the island's volcano. His extensive work in New Zealand is recognised in the Latin names of several species.

Although a very reserved individual, his friendship with leading botanists of the day (Robert Brown and William Hooker) ensured that his collections came to the attention of Charles Darwin. Many of his records and paintings are archived at the Royal Botanic Garden, Kew, the London National History Museum and St Andrews University.

Alexander Carmichael (Plate 16) was born at Taynlochan near Clachan in 1832 and was schooled by Samuel McColl at Killandrist Parish School, before going on for further education at Greenock Academy and in Edinburgh. As an exciseman, his travels in the Highlands and Islands gave him the opportunity to collect Gaelic folklore that was in danger of being lost. For over 40 years from 1855 he collected songs, prayers, blessings, charms and devotional material, first in collaboration with John Francis Campbell of Islay (1822–85) and later on his own account (Chapter 8). His unrivalled knowledge of agricultural custom and practice was called upon by the Napier Commissioners. Settling in Edinburgh, he published the first two volumes of his collection, *Carmina Gadelica*, in 1900, but he was unable to complete the enormous task of editing the remainder of the collection before his death in 1912. Nearly 30 years later, his grandson published a further two volumes, and the last two finally appeared in 1954 and 1971.

Taynlochan was also the birthplace of John McCaig (1823–1902) who had a major influence on the commercial world of Argyll and the landscape of Oban. His father, who farmed at Clachan, died when he was 11, and he and his brother Duncan sought their fortunes in Oban where they succeeded successively as drapers, tobacco manufacturers and bankers (as agents of the North of Scotland Bank). A lifelong bachelor, John amassed a considerable fortune as chairman and principal shareholder of the Oban Gas Company and owner of the North Pier. However, later generations remember him as the builder of McCaig's Folly, intended to be a replica of the Colosseum in Rome, which dominates the town from the east. Started in 1895, with the joint aims of establishing a lasting memorial to the McCaig family and providing winter work for unemployed stonemasons, the project stalled at his death in 1902. His sister Catherine, also unmarried, successfully challenged the clauses of his will that had been drafted to ensure that the building was completed. Instead, she channelled much of the family fortune into a charitable bequest fund, which continues to support good causes to the present day.

Bibliography

Carmichael, A. (1928–71) *Carmina Gadelica*. 6 vols. Edinburgh: Scottish Academic Press.

Clerk, D. (1878) 'On the Agriculture of the County of Argyll.' *Transactions of the Highland and Agricultural Society of Scotland.*

Duckworth, C.L.D. and Langmuir, G.E. (1967) *West Highland Steamers*. 3rd edn. Prescot: T. Stephenson.

Mackay, J.A. (1979) 'Islay, Jura and the Other Argyll Islands.' *Island Postal History Series*, no. 10. Published by the author at Dumfries.

Martin, C. and Martin, P. (in press). 'The Lismore Limekilns.' Report for Historic Scotland.

The Royal Commission of Inquiry into the Conditions of Crofters and Cotters in the Highlands and Islands (1884).

Stuibhart, D. (ed.) (2008) *The Life and Legacy of Alexander Carmichael*. Back, Isle of Lewis: Islands Book Trust.

Modern Times

In the twentieth century, we enter a world of fresh memories rather than dry documentary evidence. Donald Black's book *A Tale or Two from Lismore* and Margaret Lobban's book *Lachlan Livingstone and his Grandsons: Bards of Mull and Lismore* give a taste of the strong oral tradition on the island, connecting more recent experience (of family, entertainment, work, school, church and travel) with stories that stretch back to prehistory. The island museum is accumulating an extensive archive of documents (correspondence, school attendance, records of the Agricultural Society, etc.) and photographs, and a collection of the tools and things of everyday life, forming the basis for a very full social history of the last hundred years. While this is developing, this chapter completes the story of Lismore by reviewing the main milestones of the century.

World Events

Few parts of the world were able to isolate themselves from the dramatic events of the twentieth century, and Lismore had its fair share of involvement. The simple memorials outside and inside the church remind us that at least seven men from Lismore were killed in the First World War, but these were only the more obvious losses. More than 50 island men and women took an active part; their lives and their families were deeply affected. Several were wounded and discharged as unfit for military service. For example, Neil Thompson from Point, who had an adventurous career as a policeman in Ceylon and later worked as a coastguard, was seriously wounded at Passchendaele in 1918, losing his right leg below the knee. He survived to become the postmaster at Port Appin after the war but died before his time in 1934, aged 47. The influenza epidemic that arose out of the war had a particularly poignant effect, claiming the lives of two sisters, Catherine and Gertrude MacCormick, on the same day, 23 October 1918, but in two different places, Lismore and Glasgow.

Meanwhile, William Livingstone of Bachuil, who had been appointed to supervise tobacco plantations in Nyasaland (now Malawi), was caught up in the 1915 anti-colonial uprising led by John Chilembwe. Livingstone and his farm manager at Magomero, Duncan MacCormick, the 27-year-old son of the farmer at Baligarve, were both brutally murdered on 23 January. The insurgents kidnapped Livingstone's wife and children, including the infant Alastair, the future Baron of Bachuil, but they were eventually released unharmed and returned safely to live at Port Appin.

As we shall see in the next section, the post-war depression in the national economy had a serious effect on the life of the island, but the outbreak of the Second World War reaffirmed its importance as a signal post and artillery battery, protecting the many convoy vessels lying in the Linn of Lorn. Donald Black's book recaptures the spirit of these days, and there are several semi-ruinous wartime buildings on the island to testify to its strategic value to the navy.

Farming, Employment and Population

As elsewhere in the West Highlands, the Board of Agriculture provided support in the form of fresh bulls, and financial sponsorship of the annual agricultural show at Baligrundle. However, the West Highland Survey, compiled in the 1940s by Frank Fraser Darling, shows how far the farming economy on the island had declined:

> The fertility of Lismore is amazing, yet the island is poorly farmed.
> There is but little ploughing on the good rendzina soils and there
> is little breeding of stock in the proper sense of the term. The one

crofting township of sixteen crofts at Port Ramsay is composed of retired men from the sea and old folk. They let their land as grazing to a neighbouring farmer. Great numbers of cattle and sheep are bought and put on Lismore for rearing. Calves are brought in from as far afield as Carlisle, and sometimes the white scour comes along with them. Reared cattle cannot help but do well on Lismore, but rearing calves frequently have a rough time and the Director does not think that anywhere in the Highlands (except perhaps the Fort William area) has he seen calves in such a deplorable state as he has on some of the holdings on Lismore. The island, which could breed and rear the cream of cattle and sheep, is little more than accommodation ground, with an eye on Oban market. Blackface ewes are crossed with Cheviot tups and the lambs are sold off, and some good black bullocks are fattened. It is a sign of the unfortunate state of this splendid island that its 10,000 acres carry only 203 people. The cattle dealers might be sorry if there were any changes in Lismore's husbandry, but as a unit of agricultural production Lismore is nowhere near its potential. Planning in transport and produce disposal is the obvious need.

Part of the decline was caused by the collapse of markets for home-grown food in the 1920s and 1930s, but Fraser Darling underestimated the difficulties posed by the complicated state of land ownership and occupation on the island, and the lack of investment in the infrastructure of farming (steading buildings, fencing, water and electricity supplies). In the Third Statistical Account, the parish minister, Rev. Ian Carmichael, came closer to understanding the problems of land use on Lismore in the 1950s:

> In Lismore, of 84 holdings of all kinds only 15 have rentals of £50 and over, while only three have rents in excess of £100, the largest of all being £350 annually. Some of the small holdings have been sublet to the big farmers, while the holders retain their houses for dwelling purposes. Many of the islanders are not satisfied that the soil of Lismore is being used to the best purpose; they note that the distribution of the land is at present in a state of almost unbelievable confusion and that remedies are required.

However, farmers on Lismore were entering a period of improved stability and generally higher incomes. Facing severe food shortages in 1941, when thousands of tons of imports were being sunk by German U-boats, the UK government recognised the importance of home-grown meat by providing emergency financial support to hill farmers to maintain breeding stocks. With food rationing continuing after the war, this support was regularised by the passing of the Hill Farming Act (1946): 'An Act to make provision for promoting the rehabilitation of hill farming land; for the payment of subsidies in respect of hill sheep and hill cattle; for controlling the keeping of rams and ram lambs; for regulating the burning of heather and grass; for amending the law as to the valuation of sheep stocks in Scotland; and for purposes connected with the matters aforesaid.' This was the first attempt at a comprehensive policy for the fragile communities in the uplands and islands, which played an important role in maintaining national stocks of healthy and productive sheep and cattle. With the agreement of landlords, tenants were able to secure half the funding for improvements, including housing, steadings, roads, water and electricity supplies, fencing, drainage and land improvement; they also received annual cash payments based on the size of their flocks and herds.

At the same time, the pattern of farming on Lismore was changing, with the progressive replacement of horses by tractors and the associated need to invest in new machinery, but there was also progressive reduction in the amount of land ploughed each year for crops (potatoes for human consumption; oats and turnips for livestock). As it had always been difficult to secure good-quality hay in a humid and variable climate, there was a move towards conserving the grass crop as silage. Most of these changes increased the costs of production but reduced the demand for labour, resulting in greater pressure on the smaller farmer and crofter. Cross-bred lambs (Blackface x Leicester) and cattle (Highland x Shorthorn) remained the major livestock products.

The reduction in opportunities for employment on the land were matched by losses elsewhere. An unfavourable market for lime resulted in the closure of the last lime works at Sailean in 1934, by which time the prosperous days of the sailing smacks based in Port Ramsay were over. The last two, the *Mary and Effie* (Alan and Alec MacFadyen) the *Lady Margaret* (John and Dugald MacCorquodale) continued to trade until the Second World War. The smiddy closed around 1950 with the decline in demand for shoeing working horses. Meanwhile, the economy of the island was also undermined when the daily steamer service from Oban was not restored after the First World War. Subsequent developments were reported by Rev. Ian Carmichael:

> ... for over 30 years [Lismore] was served by a boat calling once a week; delivery and dispatch of mails were restricted to four days. Local protests were effective: a boat now [1958] calls twice daily on each weekday, and there is a daily delivery of mail.

Under these circumstances, it is not surprising that the population of the island continued to dwindle during the century from 500 in 1901 to just over 100 in the 1980s. What is almost unique in Lismore amongst small islands and isolated communities is the maintenance, against many odds, of a strong and living Gaelic tradition. There can be no doubt, from the evidence of the older generation, that a lively communal social life, as well as individual self-reliance, continued in the face of population decline.

New Life

Many factors have contributed to the increase in population over the last three decades to around 180 in 2008. The arrival of mains electricity in 1970 brought benefits to all aspects of life and work, and triggered widespread improvements in living conditions. Homes were better lit, there was less reliance on coal for heating and lighting, and the availability of inexpensive water pumps brought running water into some homes for the first time.

The accession of the UK into what became the European Union (EU) in 1973 meant that areas such as Lismore benefited not only from a continuation of production subsidies, now under the Common Agricultural Policy (CAP), but also from support designed to improve the infrastructure of 'less favoured areas' through 'Objective 1' status. This resulted in considerable investment, for example in fencing and farm buildings. With the most recent reform of the CAP, farm and croft subsidies are directed at enhancement of the agricultural environment, landscape and access by the public. Meanwhile there has been a modest but significant increase in the amount of land owned on a freehold basis as some of the island estates sold farms to sitting tenants, and the last few years have seen renewed interest in crofts as family units.

Nevertheless the long-term future of farming on Lismore is far from clear. There is virtually no tillage on the island, with the grassland divided between grazing and silage production, and Fraser Darling would be impressed with the quality of the cattle stock. However, in spite of genetic improvement of the Blackface breeding flocks, the island farmers still have problems with the market for small and store lambs. They continue to work at a disadvantage compared with mainland farmers because of the logistics and costs of transporting stock and feed to and from the island. Initiatives to develop 'niche marketing' of quality livestock products are hampered by the closure of the local slaughter house, resulting from EU initiatives to improve hygiene rather than welfare.

Recent years have also seen improvements in employment prospects for islanders, including the Glensanda superquarry across Loch Linnhe from Lismore, and the development of fish farming. Changes in the scheduling of the Port Appin ferry have meant that it is possible to live on the island and commute daily to work in Oban or Fort William. The island has embraced the 'IT revolution'. An initiative of Argyll and Bute Council placed a computer in every island home and financed a team of tutors to develop the skills to use them; good access to the internet has meant that well-paid work from home is now feasible. The island is fortunate that, through the lean years, it has held on to its church, primary school, nurse and shop.

These changes have brought incomers to the island but, most encouragingly, they have brought islanders back to stay and work. The new museum and café building built by the Comann Eachdraidh Lios Mòr, the renovation of the public hall, new houses going up, and the recent decision to develop the island through a community trust are signs of a renewing community.

Bibliography

Black, D. (2006) *A Tale or Two from Lismore*. Glasgow: CADISPA, University of Strathclyde.

Lobban, M.M. (2004) *Lachlan Livingstone and his Grandsons: Bards of Mull and Lismore*. Isle of Iona: The New Iona Press.

Further Reading

In addition to the bibliographies at the end of each chapter, the following publications are useful sources of information on Lismore:

Black, D. (2006) *A Tale or Two from Lismore*. Glasgow: CADISPA, University of Strathclyde.

Carmichael, I. (1947) *Lismore in Alba*. Perth: D. Leslie.

MacDonald, C.M. (ed.) (1961) Third Statistical Account of Scotland, County of Argyll. Glasgow: Collins.

McGregor, G. (1841) Second Statistical Account of Scotland. United Parish of Lismore and Appin.

McNicol, D. (1791) First Statistical Account of Scotland, vol. 1. LII. United Parishes of Lismore and Appin.

Omand, D. (ed.) (2006) *The Argyll Book*. Edinburgh: Birlinn.

Origines Parochiales Scotiae 1854. vol. iii. The Bannatyne Club. Edinburgh: W.H. Lizars.

RCAHMS (1975) *Argyll: An Inventory of the Ancient Monuments*, vol. 2: Lorn. London: HMSO.

Ritchie, G. (ed.) (1997) *The Archaeology of Argyll*. Edinburgh: Edinburgh University Press.

The most convenient point of entry to the unpublished Glenorchy, Barcaldine and Baleveolan papers relating to Lismore is:

NAS Government and private papers referring to the Isle of Lismore. Edinburgh: National Archives of Scotland.

Sources of many of the less accessible seventeenth-century records in the Glenorchy and Barcaldine papers are cited in:

Shaw, F.J. (1980) *The Northern and Western Islands of Scotland: Their Economy and Society in the Seventeenth Century.* Edinburgh: John Donald.

Copies of many of the original sources for the book can be found in the archive that is being developed at the Lismore Museum.

Index